Burned

Atlas & Co.
New York

Burned
A Memoir

Louise Nayer

Atlas & Co. *Publishers*
15 West 26th Street, 2nd floor
New York, NY 10010
www.atlasandco.com

Distributed to the trade by W. W. Norton & Company

Printed in the United States

Atlas & Co. books may be purchased for
educational, business, or sales promotional use.
For information, please write to info@atlasandco.com.

Library of Congress Cataloging-in-Publication Data
is available upon request.

ISBN: 978-1-934633-30-4

14   13   12   11   10   1   2   3   4   5   6

For my sister, Anne, in sorrow and in joy
For my parents in memory—that their story gets told
For my aunt, uncle, and cousins who gave us a home
For Jim, Sarah, and Laura
and for all the children of the world
whose lives have been irrevocably changed
in one night

Chapter One

San Francisco, CA, August 14, 1991

"It's becoming harder to drive on bridges."

"That's the effect of an anniversary reaction," explains the therapist, who is facing me in her brown leather chair. I'm sitting on the edge of my seat, clasping my chilly hands together and squeezing, as if I could squeeze out the panic.

"You're forty-two, the same age as your mother was at the time of the accident, and your daughters are the same age as you and your sister were, six and four."

"But why bridges?"

"Panic attacks often have inexplicable triggers." She sounds so reasonable.

"I was surprised to read that people who have panic attacks on bridges are afraid of stopping their car because they'll be embarrassed," I say.

I envision hundreds of cars honking at my small, white Toyota. They're trying to get home and some crazy woman has stopped her car on the Bay Bridge. It's the same, unavoidable image that's triggered each time I pass Telegraph Avenue and see the exit for Grand. Each off-ramp is farther than the next. As I reach the bridge and see traffic, the knee-jerk panic starts. Take away the red, throbbing lights on all the cars. We can't all get home in the dark. The snake of traffic is stuck, glued together and immovable. The bridge will trap me in its steely frame. Then my husband's voice: "I don't want to live with a mental health patient. Get some help." I look at my hands, expecting to see swollen veins, but for the moment I'm okay. I try to change lanes, to move left toward home and toward my husband, but I'm stuck. I can only crawl forward, along the rough and smooth patches of road. I cannot stop or get off. I feel my face tightening, my hands becoming claw-like. I stare directly ahead, determined to avoid the mirrors. I will not be overcome by dizziness, I will not feel myself detaching from the car, the road, the bridge. I have never stopped the car before.

"It sounds like you need a rest from driving. Do you need to cross the bridge this week?"

"No, I'll be in San Francisco."

But I'm so angry that a simple drive is hard. I can hear my mother: "Don't talk so much about everything."

When offered therapy herself at the time of the accident, my mother refused. "I didn't need any help. I had my friends," she'd say again and again. So after all these years, why was I still so entrenched in therapy, still trying to work through the past, break through an impenetrable wall, climb over barbed wire, when she didn't need to?

Years after the accident, my mother explained, "I didn't dwell on what could have been." Good for her, I thought to myself angrily at times. She didn't dwell, so why did I need to dwell? It's the past. Why get mired there? The perfect word for it: *mired*. Still stuck, still writing, still talking about the accident.

"I didn't want trauma victims," she told me when I asked her why we hadn't seen one of their many prominent psychiatrist friends in New York. Stella Chess visited us once and proclaimed us "fine," though many years later when I talked to her, she said she could only do so much. My mother was set against therapy.

Without help as a child—help sorting out the losses and my role in the drama, which kept unfolding—the fire took on a secret life of its own, permeating the everyday events of all of our lives. It was hard to talk about it when I was young and for many, many years later. At home, my mother referred to it only in clinical terms: the operations, the delays, the tightening of her facial skin, the difficulty swallowing. But little else was mentioned.

I had now seen my new therapist for three months and was beginning to breathe more deeply. I was beginning to believe I could make it back and forth across the bridge without fear. But the panic still flooded my system— surprising me suddenly and without warning.

Chapter Two

Wellfleet, MA, July 7, 1954

"Smell that salt spray," Daddy said, as our red Dodge pulled in front of a two-story cottage on Beach Road. It was twilight and across the narrow road a brightly lit cottage kept watch by the sea. The sea seemed to glisten especially for us, on our first family vacation.

"Well-fleet, Well-fleet." He broke up the word, letting it slip off his tongue like butter. "Everything is well with our fleet of people!" Sleepily scrunched between my big sister, Anne, and our babysitter, Della, I woke to my father's words. Small bubbles of saliva dribbled down my cheek, my brown bangs swept to the side of my high forehead. I clutched Baby, my blue-triangle-cloth doll with two painted eyes, no lips and no nose, rubbing her soft, cotton body against my cheek. Anne jumped out of the car and walked toward the house behind Daddy, grabbing his arm as he proudly strolled up to the small, bleached-white house and turned the key in the lock. "Voilà. Open Sesame," he said. Annie giggled, and they ran inside.

My mother looked at me in the backseat for a moment,

her eyes shimmering. "Isn't this a pretty little cottage?" She touched my hair for a second before she was on to something else. She had spent hours and hours searching in the newspaper for this house for us, a cottage right next to the beach where we could dip our warm bodies into the sea, where we could go on a real vacation like other doctors and their families.

"We're here," Della said. I had been leaning on her lap for hours.

Anne skipped back out of the house, ready to explore.

"Anne. Act your age," my mother said, smoothing the bottom of her yellow linen dress, "and come get things out of the car." My mother placed jump ropes and a game of Monopoly from the trunk into Annie's small arms. She raced back into the house to find Daddy.

That July day, we were far from Manhattan and the sprinklers Annie and I ran through in Playground Number Two, far from the speckled concrete that glistened in the humid New York City heat. Della was only nineteen then—far away from her friends as she lifted herself up from the sticky car seat, her long, pink skirt dragging behind her. She always wore a long skirt to cover her legs. Quietly, I got out of the back seat to follow my big sister as I always did, like a bug to the flame. My mother handed me a game of Parcheesi and a beige mesh bag of toys. Balancing a large load while clutching Baby, I walked into our summer cottage.

Everything in that Cape Cod cottage smelled of the sea: the curtains, the tops of the counters, the bathrooms, the red plaid couch, the small shelf of books. In the middle of the house, eight steep stairs led to the top bedroom. My legs were short then, and the steps were so deep that I might have fallen and gotten splinters. Daddy would have to take them out with a needle that he burned with a match, the red flame turning blue, the sulfurous smell, and then the blackened metal tip.

"I want the bed by the window," Anne yelled from the upstairs bedroom. "Weezie can have the bed next to Della." Annie was always trying to stay as far away from Della as possible. She didn't like how Della babied me, or how her cigarettes floated like missiles in the toilet.

I followed my mother outside into the twilight. She wanted to check the car. "It's pretty here," she said, closing the car door, "and so quiet at night." She pulled me toward her and lightly kissed me on the top of my head, then ruffled my hair and stroked her soft hand across my forehead, near my widow's peak, which was just like hers. At moments like that I knew I was special, yet I often felt that I was trying to catch up with her, trying to fold myself into her lemony skirts that kept disappearing.

"Sweetie, let's go inside."

"What's that door to?" I bent over, trying to lift the handles of two wooden doors laid nearly flat on the ground. I couldn't budge either one, as hard as I tried. The doors looked like they were sunk into the earth.

"Is it another room? Where I can play?"

"That's the cellar. All houses here have cellars. You must never play there, Weezie, never!"

Darkness came quickly, dropping like a long, black dress.

I climbed the steep stairs on my hands and knees to the bedroom to put Baby on my bed. I wanted her there when it was bedtime, when new shadows floated through the room that wasn't my old room anymore, the one in Peter Cooper with the predictable shadows of tree branches outside my windows. I was scared of the new house but cradled in the familiar sounds of my mother and father talking downstairs.

A foghorn sounded across the dark beach, a moaning that entered the house with a surprising strength. One at a time, I went down the stairs on my behind. Della was gazing out the window at the stars, and I sat by her to look. When my father took me uptown to the planetarium, we sat under a bowl of stars, and he showed me the Big Dipper. Sometimes there was a baseball game in the sky, with the North Star as first base. When the lights went on he said, "Stars really do hide inside the darkness. You'll see them sometime." He was right. On Cape Cod I saw more stars than I would ever be able to count in my whole lifetime. But I was afraid of the new house, its corners, its steps, its salty smell. I was afraid of the basement where I "must never play."

"Della," my mother said, "it's time for the girls to go to bed. It's too late for books." I tried to think of the morning then, something sunny, when Della brushed my hair and put it into a high pony tied with a pink ribbon.

"I'll go behind you," Della said, "so you won't fall." I crawled up the stairs. Annie had already rushed up and was opening the dresser drawer where Della had put her pajamas. I counted each step, up to eight, with Della's hand on the small of my back. "You can do it, Weezie," she said. "You're big enough. Just take it a wee bit slow."

Anne and I put on our slippered Dr. Denton pajamas and climbed into bed. My father came into the room and sat on my bed in his brown-and-white-striped cotton robe.

"We'll go to the beach tomorrow, down the wooden stairs that I showed you. Right across the street. We'll dig in the sand for sand crabs. They might be different in Cape Cod. Not like the ones at Riis Park."

"Do they live in the sand across the street?" I asked.

"Oh, even if they don't, we'll find new kinds of crabs there. Plus, we'll find clams that bury under the wet sand."

Satisfied that this was an even better place than New York, I pulled my pillow toward me, pressing my face into the starched cotton. When he reached down to kiss me, I noticed his eyes looked lighter, as if brushed clean by wings. He usually smelled of antiseptic and gauze pads, always in his black doctor bag, which he put in the hall closet next to his long woolen coat and galoshes. Today he smelled like the salt wind blowing through the open window. He pulled the covers tightly over me, cocooning me inside the fresh sheets.

"Stay, Daddy. Please." I reached up and touched his face. "Your chinny chin chin," I said, laughing and holding my hand there, his whiskers scratching my palms.

"I need to say goodnight to Annie and unpack and check out our new house. Your mother and I have things to do."

My mother came in to sit on my bed. "Get a good night's sleep, sweetie pie." Her silky hand brushed my hair from my forehead. At night my mother's eyes turned into dark jewels and her skin became soft and peachy, all the tight corners of her features gone.

"Don't go to work, Mommy." I reached for her hands. How easily our fingers fit together. "And don't talk about being a nurse. Promise?"

"It's nighttime." She kissed me on the forehead. "Daddy and I won't be going to work for this whole vacation."

"Oh yay, yay, yay!" I threw my arms around her neck and held them there, gently fingering the delicate white-lace trim of her nightgown. I held on tight.

"Go to sleep, my baby, go to sleep. Go to sleep, my baby. Go to sleep." She sang the song she always sang to me at night.

"Sing it again and again and again," I said.

"Goodnight, sweetie pie. Sleep tight. I need to say goodnight to Annie." She loosened my grip on her hands.

"I'm scared of monsters!"

"Goodnight, Weezie. Nothing bad is going to happen."

"Don't go so far away."

"You'll be fine," she said, laughing. "We're just downstairs. Now go to sleep." Her voice was firm.

"Peachy pie, goodnight." My mother moved to Annie's bed, a small dent on my blanket the only evidence that she had been next to me. She kissed Annie and walked down the steep stairs. My father and Annie talked for a long time. He explained how a bay is formed and which side of the island has the ocean waves. She kept asking questions, questions I didn't know how to ask. He drew a small map, gave her a final kiss, and left. The room emptied too quickly. Della was not upstairs yet.

"Are you awake, Annie?" I looked over to where my big sister lay sprawled out, one foot under the covers and the other out.

"A bit. But I don't want to talk now. Tomorrow. Go to sleep, Weezie."

"But there are monsters on the ceiling, in all sorts of shapes, like dinosaurs, the ones with the teeth."

"Those are shadows from the curtains. Go to sleep."

I thought of all the shadows in the churches that Della took me to. It was always cold in the churches, and I stayed right next to her skirt. She lit candles in little glass cups. Sometimes she said out loud whom each candle was for while I stared at scenes of the Virgin Mary cradling baby Jesus as the smell of wax and incense swirled around us.

Now, curled up into a little ball, I leaned my back against the wall and listened to the sea. Annie fell asleep quickly. My parents' voices rose up the stairs.

"I hope the hurricane loses its power before it hits the Cape, goddamnit," my father said.

"Don't worry so much, darling. It's not even raining and there are no storm warnings, only predictions. You're always making something out of nothing!"

The sound of the waves on the sand drew me toward

sleep as the white curtains swayed back and forth. Finally, Della came up the stairs, got into her pajamas, and crawled into the bed next to mine. I liked to hear her breathing next to me. In New York she often went out for a few hours to Sam's Pizza on 14th Street with the Irish girls she knew and some of the security guards. She wanted Frank, who patrolled near 2 Peter Cooper, to like her. I heard her talk about him in the dark stairwell of our building where I sat with her on some afternoons. That night, she whispered in the dark to God, praying that some day she would have a family of her own, little children and a handsome husband, though I knew she worried about the acne scars that spread all over her face. I wished that I could fix them, smooth them over like cookie batter.

I heard my father close the windows downstairs. His feet padded across the floor. And I heard my mother preparing for bed, the water spinning down the sink as she washed her pretty face just as she always did, with a clean, soft washcloth.

Chapter Three

Only a week after we arrived in Wellfleet, my father woke us early to go clam digging before breakfast. We crossed Beach Road and went down the steps next to our neighbor's house and onto the sand.

"Find the bubbles," my father said as we started digging. I looked for the miniscule air pockets, small miracles like seeds that grew into flowers. I loved to feel the warm sand between my toes, and let it slide through my fingers. I loved the colored grains, where I hoped to find live creatures. My fingers brushed against small pieces of shells and the slimy seaweed that wound around them like thick, green rings. When we got home, my father ate the clams, as slimy and slippery as frogs. Then he lit up his Lucky Strikes.

"Isn't it disgusting—these slimy clams?" he teased, putting his arm around my mom, smoke curling between them. Annie and I gagged in playful disgust. Della put out orange juice in plastic green-and-white-flecked cups. I dumped a heaping spoonful of brown sugar into my cereal bowl. My mother turned the other way and then looked back at me and smiled. We both loved sweets. Brown sugar coated all my teeth.

"Diddy, Diddy," Annie said. "What are you reading?"

"There's a new polar bear at the Central Park Zoo." Annie ran over to his side of the table, claiming him all to herself. He read her the whole story—when the polar bear arrived, his size, where he came from—and they talked until I got bored and tapped my foot hard against the chair.

"Stop making so much noise," my mother said. "You have to learn patience." Then her voice softened. "Soon we'll read some books. Della, help the girls change into clothes for the library."

"Please can I wear this lacy shirt?" I begged Della.

"No, Weezie, too fancy." I sighed and picked a red T-shirt. Della slipped it over my head even though I could do it myself. Having Della pamper me was my way of getting back at Annie for using words like "visibility" and for asking my father questions about clams, questions that were forming on my lips like bubbles that burst when she asked them before I could. When we came downstairs, my mother told me to tuck in my shirt. She then wet a washcloth and wiped off some remnants of sugar that had caked at the sides of my mouth. She tried to wipe off Annie's face, too, but Annie ran away from her toward the car.

"Anne. Come back here now and let me clean your face if you want to go into town. You can't look like a mess at the library!"

Annie dragged herself back inside and my mother cleaned her off.

"That's better. Now you look presentable!"

Della stayed at home while the four of us rode into town down windy, narrow roads. "In the blink of an eye," my mother said about small towns that quickly came and went. Wellfleet was a blink-of-an-eye town. We dropped my mother off by the row of shops; she wanted to look in the windows before meeting us for lunch in an hour. Then my father parked the car next to the library. There were no long steps or lions like at the library in New York. This library was one big room with big windows so the light poured over the table at its center.

The librarian knew us by then. "We're up from Manhattan," my father had told her last week, "and we'll be coming in every few days to get books for the children." Today he asked her if anything new had come in. I loved the way he talked, easy like the way he walked.

I ran over to the section with all the Peter Rabbit books that my mother loved. The rabbits wore vests and had fluffy tails. My sister picked *Curious George*.

At the restaurant, I slipped off the booth like a slide and landed under the table where it was dark and cool. I pulled Annie's leg and she giggled and messed up my hair. My mother had gone to the bathroom.

"Weezie!" she said in her firm voice when she returned. "Get out from under the table. Don't you want a hot dog and French fries? Hank, why did you let her get herself all dirty! The floor's not sanitary." My father was quiet. I don't think he even noticed that I had slid off my seat.

After we ate, my mother opened up a small package and gave each of us a small, wooden jewelry box. Mine had a red rose on the front, with a green stem that circled the bottom of the box. Annie's had a yellow rose.

"Oh Mommy, it's beautiful," Anne said, opening it and touching the red velvet inside.

"Thanks, Mommy." I fingered the red rose and stem. I wondered if she would let me keep my shells from the beach in the box.

At home, Della had made our beds, put out our swimsuits on top of our pillows, and placed our beach pails and shovels by the front door.

We crossed the road with Daddy, who wore dark sunglasses, descended the steps again, spread out our beach towel and sat down to read. Later, Annie and I collected seashells along the beach to put on a small shelf in our bathroom. We came back to the towel and spilled our treasures onto the striped cotton. Suddenly Anne ran down to the sea as if someone had yelled her name. My father rose up in his thin legs and screamed at her to come back, but when she didn't, he grabbed my hand and we rushed down to the water. I stayed by the edge, away from the danger, the water running over my toes, and he leapt into it toward Anne, yelling, "Come back to the edge, goddamnit!" She came in to where the froth gathered around her ankles and looked at him with pure joy.

"Don't ever do that again! You could drown."

I took Annie's hand and we raced to our beach towel, to our mother, who had come down from the cottage for a short time. She had brought the white plastic lemonade cooler and crustless sandwiches, which she unwrapped one by one, careful to keep the bread free of sand. A little bit of pulp floated in the sugary drink. I tasted the lemon sugar that mixed with the salt on my lips. Sweet and sour. My mother held me close for a few minutes, talked with my father, and then went back to the cottage.

The next day, Annie crossed the street to Liberty Winters' house, the parakeet-yellow house with the wind chimes. Liberty and Anne played for hours. They would fly across the mattresses that lay all over Liberty's basement floor. I was alone with my mother since my father had gone into town and Della was resting. I wanted my mother to talk to me or hold me in her arms.

In cleaning mode, she put Bon Ami on a sponge and wiped the counters until they gleamed. My mother liked the word "gleam," and her lips pursed like those of a proper English woman, which she was, since her own mother had arrived alone on a boat from England at seventeen. My mother had England in her blood, in her hair, and in the tea she drank every day. Her skin was cream-colored. She liked fresh cream and strawberries, English muffins, and honey in the comb. She once remarked that an apartment building near where we lived in New York looked like her honeycomb, all the little apartments with windows. If I was lucky, she would hold me on her lap and put her soft cheek next to mine, cooing, "Sweetie pie. You are my sweetie pie." If she wasn't too busy, she might read me a book. Today she read to me from *Peter Rabbit*. She loved Peter Rabbit and showed me the shiny pictures. I knew that he slipped past the evil when he didn't become minced pie. I wanted her to read that part over and over, how he slipped past the evil.

It was almost lunchtime now, and she made small, triangle-shaped sandwiches, cutting off the crusts and throwing them into the wastebasket. I thought of the poor children in Della's Ireland and wanted to pick out the brown edges and send them through the mail in envelopes that I could lick with my tongue.

I got bored and watched the flies that landed on the windowsill, their tiny back legs whirring up and down in the air, their black heads and bodies turning light red or yellow. Sometimes they attached themselves to the venetian blinds and remained there, perfectly still.

"This house is so small, everything shows," my mother said with a sigh. I could see how clean the gold-and-yellow-speckled linoleum was when I peered down past my legs. Everything was clean and neat and put-together, even the tips of my mother's rose-colored fingers. I looked out the kitchen window to Liberty's house across the street and wanted to fly across the mattresses that lay all over their basement floor.

"Your mom and dad are going out tonight," Della said as we washed our hands in the small upstairs bathroom before dinner, surveying our new multicolored seashells that sat on the window ledge.

"I like it when Daddy reads to me," Anne said. "Diddy, Diddy, Diddy."

"Well, you can't have everything you want. You and Weezie have it easy." Annie dried her hands and turned around, glaring at Della. I followed my sister to the top of the stairs while Della huffed down the steps in front of us to the living room, where my parents were reading.

"I'm sure Della already told you," my mother said. "We're going to a play in Provincetown. But you need to go to bed right after books. Tomorrow is a busy day. We're going to the beach in the morning and then driving into town for lunch."

"Can I get a sundae?" I asked.

"Sure, sweetie, with vanilla ice cream and butterscotch. But no sundae unless Della says you got to bed on time," she replied, folding the paper and placing it neatly on the coffee table. I hated how everything always depended on something else.

Della moved to the kitchen and took out a saucepan from under the kitchen cabinet to prepare macaroni and cheese, while Anne and I sat on the floor by the coffee table and began coloring. The pilot light was out on the burners.

"I called the gas company," my mother said to Della. "Fix the children a snack and then they can eat when the stove is fixed."

To my father, she said, "Dear, the gas company says they'll send someone to fix the stove at 6 p.m. They'll deliver the new tanks and relight the pilot light. Della can let them in."

"I don't like them coming here when we're gone, damn it."

"Stop it," she said firmly, putting her finger to her lips to silence him. "Again, you're being a worrywart!" They both went into the bedroom and shut the door.

"Can I get that for you?" I heard him zip up her dress. Anne and I pressed our ears to the door.

"You look pretty in that, darling." Then we heard a

kiss, a smack of lips, as Della came and shuffled us back to the kitchen.

"You look pretty in that, darling," we whispered to each other, dancing in circles with our arms around each other. "Pretty, pretty, pretty."

When my mother and father came out of the bedroom, they looked like a king and queen, the sound of elegant fabric brushing against the small table next to the living room couch. My father glanced at my mother, who placed a lace handkerchief, initialed D.D.N. for Dorothy Dennison Nayer, into her summery wicker purse. She wore a white linen dress threaded with tiny cream-colored fish. Over the dress a thick, crocheted, lavender shawl swept her shoulders like a wave. I didn't want them to go out that night or any night. I didn't even want them in the bedroom downstairs. But they looked so beautiful, they belonged someplace else, beyond doorways in small cottages on beach roads. They belonged in castles, in mirrored hallways, on red velvet couches, in rooms flooded with gold like the sun.

My mother reached down to kiss me and I felt her lips on my cheeks. I had reached up to touch her own soft cheeks that afternoon on the beach, lying in her lap, melting into her like butter on toast. Her rose perfume swirled around her like the incense in the church, a flowery scent that stayed in the room for hours. After she kissed us, red lipstick smudged our cheeks.

"Hold on a second, I'll wipe it off." She wet her fingertips and carefully wiped it off, first Anne and then me.

My dad had his arm lightly around my mother's shoulder now. He wore a light-blue seersucker suit and navy tie, so different from the morning attire when he wore only bathing trunks to walk with us on the beach. He kissed us both, his face clean-shaven and shiny, and they walked out the door.

Soon after my parents left the house, a man knocked loudly on the door, startling all three of us.

"It's the gas company." Della let him in, a blond man with dancing blue eyes and tools hanging off his belt.

"I'll take the old tank in back and replace it. Then I'll relight the stove. You must be hungry for dinner. I ran into the Mr. and Mrs. on the road a few minutes back, and hello to you children."

Della put her hands on her hips and talked in a lilting voice, like she did with the security guards in their navy uniforms and stiff hats at Peter Cooper. He went out the back, the tools clanging against his body. When he returned, Anne and I stood in our pink Dr. Denton pajamas with the feet that stuck to the floor and watched him light the pilot light.

"All ready to roll. Wait about five minutes until you use the stove, though. Then everything will be fine."

After he left, darkness descended and a chill wind rushed in through the cracks underneath the door. Della made macaroni and cheese. Then we went to the living room couch where she read *The Merbaby* to us.

Across the street, the waves held their breath before they broke. I heard the foghorns too, and saw the mist settling on the sun-blistered houses. The air, even inside, was wet and salty. I reached up and touched my sun-burned face.

When Della finished the story, we were content that the fisherman and his wife cuddled a human baby of their own, while the Merbaby with the human face and fish tail, whom they had rescued and loved, was now back in the sea, united with her sisters.

"Tomorrow, you will go into town, so you need your bit of rest." Della led us up the steep stairs to our beds.

She perched at the edge of my bed, bent down to kiss me, and then sang, "In Dublin's fair city, where the girls are so pretty, I first laid my eyes on sweet Molly Malone, as she wheeled her wheelbarrow, through streets broad and narrow, crying cockles and muscles, alive, alive o."

At night, Della saw ghosts in the walls. I could see them too, gauzy strings of light.

"It creaks more than the city house," Della said, and sighed. "You'll catch your bit of cold, Weezie." She pulled a thick blanket over me and then checked on Annie, who turned her head away when Della tried to kiss her. Anne didn't like the stale smell of cigarettes that stuck to Della's skin, her red paisley kerchiefs, and her face pockmarked with acne scars. Della smudged beige makeup over the pockets in her cheeks, but nothing seemed to work.

Just like tiny swimming pools, I thought, looking at Della's face, tiny pools with nothing inside them. Annie said that when Daddy was a doctor in the war, he had a patient who was a young man with smallpox. Daddy saved his life, but the man had holes in his face forever. He never got vaccinated. We had holes in our thighs from the vaccination, so we wouldn't have holes in our faces. Annie showed me mine, how if I ran my finger over my leg, it would suddenly touch a shiny circle.

"When are Mommy and Daddy coming home?" I asked Anne. She turned her face toward mine.

"Not for a while, but we have to keep listening for the car. I know that sound. Just listen."

I sat up for a minute, cupping my hands over my ears, imagining my parents coming home all dressed up, but all I could hear was the sound of the waves breaking.

"Tomorrow, we can wear our new dotted Swiss dresses with the velvet sashes that Mommy made us when we go to town," Anne said. "I'm having a hot fudge sundae and you're having butterscotch, right?"

"Right. Do you want your cherry?"

"No. You can have it."

"I wish Mommy and Daddy were home. Let's stay up."

"I'll try, but I'm tired."

"Well I'm not. So I'll stay up and wake you up. I'm counting to eight and back."

Downstairs, Della always sat on the couch and turned on the radio. Only a few channels came through, but she said she liked to drown out the sounds of the foghorns and the waves crashing. Human voices soothed her, though the Boston accent made her laugh. My father sometimes imitated the A sounds—"I pahked my cah in Hahvad yahd"—while eating his breakfast.

The house smelled of dishwashing detergent, Bon Ami, and the salty air. I drifted in and out of sleep, but I woke to hear Della trudge up the stairs, change into her long-sleeved, pink, flannel pajamas and enter our small, shadowy room with three beds. Sometimes she liked to stare at us at night. It was because she wanted her own children. She said that I always cradled my head in my cupped hands as if I was holding my dreams, and Annie slept on her back with her arms spread wide like an angel, open to the sky and fearless.

Chapter Four

"It's past midnight," my mother said to my father. "The girls will be up early, asking you to take them clam digging." My mother leaned comfortably on the couch at the home of the Fairchilds, friends they visited after dinner and a play.

Rising from the couch, my father reached out his hand to pull my mother up to him. He smelled her rose perfume and for that very moment believed he was the luckiest man alive. His fingers touched the gold of her small wedding band.

When he had first met her, he had been struck by her loveliness and her spirit. She was so alive! Throughout his four years at Yale, while others were going to football games, movies, and weekend parties, he hid in his room studying. He had a girlfriend from Paterson whom he kept in touch with during freshman year, a kind, pretty girl who adored him. But as he was surrounded by Ivy League men and their fancy dates, and later by nurses at Mt. Sinai—bright, ambitious women who kept up with the latest medical treatments—he called her less and she lost hope that they would get married.

He met my mother through the secretary at Columbia's Teachers College, who seemed to have a matchmaker's talent and an endless curiosity about who was with whom. They ended up at the same party and when he left with her that night, aware that something big might be happening, he was so preoccupied with talking about his brother's death that he forgot to put a token in the turnstile for her on the subway. He was also wearing galoshes, which she kept looking at with a mixture of amusement and undoubtedly a degree of disgust. But he did manage to get her phone number, and she agreed to see him again, though she wondered if he was just a dud with no manners.

On their second date, he sensed how proper she was and admired her lacy gloves and black velvet hat. Just a touch of rouge covered her cheeks, and her velvety eyes shone. Her clothes were impeccable, tailored with matching purse and shoes. Along with her clothes and good looks, he somehow felt more complete in her presence. Though she rarely talked about her past, he sensed in her a kindred soul.

They married quickly. My mother was a war bride. They had a small civil service, and she wore a red woolen suit with a revealing V-neck trimmed with layers of white lace that framed her face like huge, white petals. He bought her a small diamond ring, nervously picking it out only a few days before the wedding. My mother's brother, Louis, and his wife, Rusty; my mother's parents, Fanny and Joseph Daubert; and my father's cousin, Frieda, all attended the ceremony and went to the White Turkey restaurant. My parents had pulled it off: they were married. Like so many other men at the time, he could go away to war knowing his wife was waiting for him.

While he worked as a physician in Persia, he dreamed every day of my mother and their life-to-be. In 1946, when the boat returned to New York Harbor, my mother waited anxiously on the dock, watching the Moran tugboats pull the ship to safety, returning her husband to her.

He helped her drape her lavender shawl over her shoulders. They walked arm in arm through the chilly evening air to the red Dodge.

"I'll drive, darling," she said.

"Of course." He was relieved that she'd pilot the car. He had night blindness. The lines in the road ran together and dissolved after twilight.

"Look at how dark the water looks, dear, spotted white with moonlight."

"I'm driving. I can't look at the water." Her hands were steady on the wheel.

"Of course not." He put his left arm around her neck. She leaned her head back slightly, and he caressed her wispy hair in his palm and the downy skin of her neck, as the wet, salty air rushed into the car. Out the window, thousands of stars pierced the dark.

They drove for the next half hour in a humid silence, aware of each other, aware of the stars, aware of the long stretch of water on their right as they passed small cottages, all the lights off except for maybe one or two porch lights. Miles away Annie and I slept soundly upstairs with Della. We were beach children that night; nothing could completely wash out the tiny bits of mineral-rich sand and salt water from our bodies. We slept with the sound of the waves and woke to the sight of the sea, all the shades of green, blue, and black like a bruise the size of the world.

It was almost 1:00 a.m. when the car pulled in front of the cottage, right next to a small patch of green lawn. My mother turned off the ignition. My father climbed out of the car and gently closed the car door so as not to disturb anyone inside the house.

"There's no hot water, Hank," my mother said after putting on her pale green nightgown, the one with the lace neck. She held her thin hands under the bathroom faucet, waiting for the water to turn warm. Only cold water washed over her fingers.

"Just keep it running. This is the country, dear."

"I've already been here a few minutes. We've got to do something. I bet the gas company forgot to light the pilot light downstairs when they delivered the propane."

"Dorothy, calm down. This can wait." His voice rose. "This is not what I've planned for the end of the evening. To fix a hot water heater!"

"You know I always wash my face before bed. Where are the matches? Where is the flashlight? I'm going down to the cellar."

"The matches are there—in the drawer. The flashlight is there, too. But this is silly. It's after midnight!"

"I don't care!"

She walked quickly to the kitchen, already searching through the kitchen drawer and finding the book of matches from The Town Crier, where the whole family had eaten the week before. She was annoyed that my father didn't take charge, that she had to do it. That's why she moved so fast, like a locomotive that my father couldn't stop.

"Here, Hank. You hold the flashlight."

"Look. Hold up, will you," he said, exasperated, his Dorothy already out the door. He followed her in his bathrobe, the chilly air raising the black hairs on his arms. He had no time to notice the dome of stars and the bright moon above, for she had already opened the cellar door, leaving the two handles buried in the earth, and was climbing furiously down the wooden ladder in the pitch black. With the rungs so far apart, she almost slipped, and her calves ached when she got to the basement floor.

"Slow down. I'm worried. That's all we need, for you to break a bone!"

"Stop being such a worrywart!"

Both down the rickety ladder, they were enveloped in darkness, except for the beam of his light. The basement smelled of mold, of wet walls and musty things growing, taking over, and they could hear a hum, the buzzing of the house.

"Isn't there a light switch here?" she asked.

"Look, I've got the light. The flashlight. That's all the light we have."

He held it up, making sure to leave the door to the cellar open. He never liked enclosed spaces, where he felt crushed like bruised fruit.

My mother, only five-feet-two, was strong, fast, and impatient, just wanting to get the task over with so she could wash her face, put the warm washcloth over her forehead, her eyes, her cheeks, her chin and watch the dirt trickle down the drain. She walked to the right side of the dark room where the water heater stood, an old and rusty cylinder, prematurely aged by salty air. Goose bumps covered her bare arms.

My father, feeling exposed in all the dampness, moved to the right toward my mother, the ties on his bathrobe having come loose.

"Point the flashlight here," she said, as if talking down to a child. "No, not like that! Didn't you ever learn anything about how to fix a house?"

He wasn't listening to her; he was trying to smell something, to take his time, to think about what to do next. He was a medical officer for the New York City Fire Department. He knew about these things.

"Shine your light next to the valve. I'll have to turn it on after I light the match," my mother said, but my father was trying to remember words, echoes of phrases the New York City fireman said to him about pilot lights, gas heaters, testing the pipes with soap bubbles.

"Hank. Come back from dreamland. This is where I need to light it." She was annoyed that his mind drifted so far away, as if he wasn't listening to her.

"Wait a minute, damn it, will you. Let's look at this together," but before he could get the words out, my mother in her lime-green nightgown with the white lace neck had already turned on the valve and lit the match from the red matchbook that had sat in a small blue bowl at the restaurant in Provincetown—the same bright red book of matches that I had tried to snatch up until my mother told me I wasn't allowed to play with them; the same matches that Annie had said she was old enough to take home until my mother took them away from her, too; the same book of matches that my father had put in his pocket to light up his Lucky Strikes after the meal.

When the red tip of the match struck against the edge of the matchbook, there was the familiar, ordinary sound of the strike—and the spark ignited: an instantaneous explosion like a one-syllable scream, then silence. Engulfed in flames, not even the damp, growing specks of mold on the wall, the ocean across the street, or the salty air could stop the blue flames of the inferno from scorching their skin. The searing pain flung them to the ground. The gas that had no smell had been escaping for hours.

Above ground, the foghorn beckoned ships lost at sea. Della, Annie, and I slept upstairs. We didn't hear our car park on the small patch of lawn. We didn't hear my father turn the key in the lock when my parents entered the house. We didn't hear the flash fire down below.

Escaping the inferno was like ascending a hill of hot molasses. My father—his hands, face, chest, and neck flaming—climbed up the ladder first. He lifted himself into the hole of sky, the loose tie on his brown-and-white-striped bathrobe burning, then his pajamas, and then his skin—all in an instant.

My mother followed him, the skin of her face raw blisters, exploding with fire. "Hank!" she cried out desperately. She wished my dad was behind her, that his bones could propel her to safety and take the wild burning off her face, neck, hands, and legs.

"Hank!" she screamed as she knocked her hands against the ladder, knocking them harder on each rung so the fire would disappear, but her legs were on fire and felt like leaden weights. Each time she put a hand up, she hit the other hand against her face to stop the agony. She reached upward, in excruciating pain, wondering if she would get to the next rung or collapse, fall back from the fragile spider web of a ladder into the inferno and die. My father's moans filled the air.

"Help! Help!" He rolled on the lawn, rolling and rolling out the fire and the pain.

When my mother climbed out of the cellar and reached the lawn, she, too, dropped her burning body on the now singed lawn and tried to roll away the pain, her green nightgown charred, her face burned to the bone.

"Help! Help!" my father yelled, but no one answered.

"Help!" my mother shrieked, collapsed on the burnt grass, the cellar now an empty socket of fire.

Chapter Five

I was sleeping soundly, my body pressed to the wall in soft folds of pajamas. Suddenly, footsteps thundered up the stairs. Della lifted me off the pressed sheets with their perfectly angled hospital corners; her face was ashen, her pupils as huge as saucers, as if she had finally seen the ghost hidden in the blistered cottage walls. I put my arms around her wet and slippery neck.

"We're going across the street. Get up. To Liberty's." She talked loud and fast.

"Why?" Anne said, bolting upright and rubbing her eyes. "Where are Mommy and Daddy?"

"Just follow me. No questions."

Anne threw off her covers, swung her legs over the side of the bed and rushed down the stairs without putting on her slippers. She went to find Mommy and Daddy.

"Your slippers," I said. "Mommy always says to . . . " but my voice faded as my arms sealed themselves around Della's neck so hard that she had to loosen my hold. Her thick tears dripped on my arm. I had never seen her cry before. I shivered.

"Mommy! Daddy!" Anne shrieked as she stumbled down the stairs. "Mommy! Daddy!" Her eyes were wild now, her pupils inky and dilated. Strange men lumbered in and out of the cellar, boots pounding the floor, loud voices echoing from the pit below.

Annie ran into the empty bedroom: the door open, the beds perfectly made, Daddy's brown shoes next to his side of the bed, the laces hanging down.

"Shush, Shush," Della said, grabbing Anne's hand and pulling her toward her. We raced out of the front door. In the cold night, I clutched my arms tighter around Della's wet neck, felt her clutching me, her arms around my waist. The freezing air stung my sunburned face. The stars appeared flattened in the sky, flat as paper. The chilly air quivered down my neck. Anne bleated now like a small, injured lamb. Della's tears dripped on my face, and I tasted the salt. As we crossed the street to Liberty's house, I looked back at our summer cottage. Men in silver suits and large hoods moved like armored insects in the cellar. A thick, smoky scent mixed with the salt-water air.

The small pole in front of our house was draped with something half burned. Even in the darkness, Annie and I could see it.

"Daddy's bathrobe." Annie kept sucking in her breath and not breathing out, like when she had asthma in the middle of the night. "That's my daddy's bathrobe. Daddy, Daddy, Daddy!"

Della rushed us into Liberty's house. My stomach hurt, jabs of pain pierced me as we went through Liberty's door, down the stairs into the basement room full of mattresses where we always pretended to fly like Peter Pan. "Make a magic wish," we had whispered just yesterday, hurling ourselves from bed to bed. "If you make a wish you can fly, fly, fly!" *Candy, Santa Claus. The beach.*

The room was damp and moldy; perfectly rounded, green spores stuck to the top of the ceiling. I crawled into an old, gray sleeping bag with Della near me and plugged my ears. Anne screamed again. She half sat, half slumped on one of the mattresses next to Liberty. Her cries were punching out my insides. I wanted her to stop. I wanted her to fix everything. I wanted her to bring back my mother and father.

Suddenly we heard a car pull up, the engine die down. Annie and I stared at each other. It had to be our parents returning. Liberty's mother walked slowly into the house. Her eyes were dull sockets. She held my sister hard and sang to her. But nothing would console her. I wanted my mother and father so badly my skin hurt. I wanted to go across the street. I didn't want this night ever to have happened.

Della played with the pink ribbon in my hair, twirling it in her fingers like she did with her rosary beads. "They'll be back in a week." She looked at the wall, not at Anne and me. "They were burned a little."

"You're lying," Anne said. "Lying."

Mrs. Winters held Anne's hand until she sobbed herself to sleep. I stayed up, rubbing my hand over my stomach, around and around. Why would my mother and father leave without even saying good-bye? Why would they forget me? Tears filled my eyes and tumbled soundlessly down my face.

The next morning a ray of sun cut through the small window like a sword. I was surprised to be in a sleeping bag on an old mattress in the basement of another house, my parents gone. Della was sleeping next to me with her mouth open, breathing hard. And it looked like she still had her jacket on, or maybe it had just been thrown helplessly over her. I smelled her Camel cigarette breath. Annie was all curled up asleep next to Liberty. In the dark night Annie had screamed and screamed and I had clamped my hands over my ears for hours until her voice stopped. I held onto that warmth now—my hands on my ears. I wanted to hear the sea inside, like Daddy showed me with a big shell.

"Will Daddy take us to the beach today?" I asked Della as she lifted her heavy body off the bed, her red wool sweater spilling onto the cool basement floor. "Will Daddy take us to the beach today?"

"They were hurt—in an accident." Her face was puffed up and red. I turned away, clutching my stomach, an acid taste rising in my mouth.

"They'll be back in seven days."

"You're lying!" Anne yelled from the bed, suddenly uncurling from her catlike position.

"Liar, liar, Della. You're lying!"

"Anne, shush. Your mother wouldn't like that kind of talk."

"My mother's not here! Diddy. Where are you? Diddy. Diddy. Diddy."

Again, I cupped my hands over my ears.

"Stop upsetting Weezie, Anne."

Anne jumped out of bed, tightened her jaw and marched up the stairs with Liberty trailing behind her.

Della was crying. I wanted to be dead like a stone and pulled the covers over my head.

Chapter Six

Upstairs, at Liberty's wooden breakfast table, Annie and I stared at our cereal bowls. The cornflakes drowned in a sea of milk. I excused myself to throw up a smelly brown liquid in the bathroom. Anne stopped crying and stopped asking questions. I needed her. I needed to be next to her. I stood by her all the time, even when she tried to get away from me, treating me as if I were a reminder. She kept looking far away, like a lighthouse. Where were our parents? Why didn't they call us on the telephone?

We were both staring out the window, the hot sun high in the sky, when Aunt Peggy, our mother's best friend, drove up to our cottage. She talked to Della, who was outside packing the car, and then rang the bell to Liberty's house. When she came inside, Annie and I stood still, as if waiting for instructions. Then she came to us, her red hair in a bun, her blue eyes wet as she gathered us in her large, pink skirt.

"Girls," she said, "girls, girls." Her arms wrapped around us. "I'll drive you to the Simons. Remember Dr. Simon and his wife, Bitten, from Bound Brook Island? Their son, Johnny, is there. In a while you'll see your Uncle Louis."

Her words rushed over me like tears. I couldn't remember the Simons and their son, Johnny. My head felt like it was filled with mud, dark and slippery. Thoughts got scrambled then flew away.

"I just want Mommy and Daddy," I said, as soft as the sheer white curtain in our cottage bedroom.

"They'll be back soon," Aunt Peggy lied. I knew it was a lie, but I didn't know what was behind the curtain of her voice. I wanted to hear my mother's voice, but nothing was being promised.

Aunt Peggy left.

We looked out the window again. Annie had her elbows on the windowsill and her face squished against the glass. I tried to hold on to Annie's arm, but she had to go to the bathroom, and I cried when she left me. After she came out, I went into the bathroom and threw up again, the same acid-metal taste in my mouth. Liberty's mom wiped off my face with a soft washcloth. "There, there," she said, scooping up the bad smell. "There, there."

She wanted me to lie down, but I wanted to stay by Annie. Annie must know more than I do, I thought. She will tell me what really happened. If I am quiet and good, and throw up silently and clean the outside of the toilet with a tissue and flush it down deep, she'll tell me that my parents will return. I started counting, counting my fingers, counting my toes, counting the sparkles in the linoleum, counting the number of blue veins in my hands.

Liberty moved through the house back and forth. She tried to get us to play, bringing out dolls, her flowered plastic tea sets, paints and an easel, but my sister wouldn't budge from her place at the window. I sat there next to her and Liberty tried to find her place between us.

Out the window we watched Della continue to pack the car with our things: our suitcases, the mesh bag with our toys that Anne had helped bring into the house when we arrived, the game of Parcheesi that my mother made me carry, our pails and shovels still lightly coated with sand from the beach, and our stuffed animals.

Liberty stared at the floor, holding one of the dolls we always played with, stroking the long, brown hair too hard with her fingers so that small strands fell on the floor. Then she ran into her bedroom and brought out two bottle caps. She gave one to each of us. I put mine into my pants pocket, but it hurt my leg when I walked. Mrs. Winters walked us out to the car.

In the blinding sunlight, we both stared, open-mouthed, at Daddy's burned bathrobe. Daddy's bathrobe, my daddy, the shell of my daddy draped across the wooden pole, burned in the middle like the thin pieces of carbon paper in my mommy's desk drawer. I wanted him to come back inside his robe. I didn't want him to fall apart. Where was he? Where was Mommy's robe? Aunt Peggy kissed us on our foreheads and forced a smile. Della hugged us hard for a long time. She would take a bus back to the city.

As we drove for a long time to the Simons' house on Bound Brook Island, I couldn't get the image of the robe out of my mind and kept pinching myself to make it go away.

"Are we getting closer or farther away from Mommy

and Daddy?" Anne asked Aunt Peggy again and again. "Closer or farther away?" She was playing the "hot and cold" game. If you say "hot," you're near. If you say "cold," you're far away.

"They're in a hospital nearby. Not too far away. Look at how pretty the sea is today, sparkling blue. Maybe you can swim later. Your swimsuits are right at the top of the suitcase, all ready to go."

When my mother and father arrived at the Cape Cod Hospital, no one working there was prepared for the injuries they had sustained. Mrs. Winters had found them rolling on the lawn, my father half naked, my mother's polyester nightgown stuck to her scorched skin. Mrs. Winters, with Della's help, put them into the back of her car, wrapped them in blankets, and tried not to gag as she drove a mile down the road to the doctor's house while Della sat with us in the basement room. The doctor immediately called a Cape Cod ambulance. Most of the sleepy vacationers probably didn't even hear the sirens. For some, the sounds might have been a momentary awakening, a memory of the big city they had left.

At the small Cape Cod hospital, the nurse had to stop herself from gagging at the sight of the raw, red, blistering burns, and the putrescent smell of burned flesh that enveloped the room. The young doctor on duty had been chatting with the nurse, commenting on the slow night, when my parents arrived. He had to breathe deeply, past where his voice stuck in his throat, and remember everything he had ever learned about burn victims. Fortunately, he remembered a paragraph with a hideous photograph in his medical book, which showed how you must always remove the clothing first. He cut off my mother's thin, green nightgown already sticking to her skin, reminiscent of the way the flowers on the kimonos of the Hiroshima victims burned onto their backs. The nurse tossed the nightgown in the garbage while the doctor removed my mother's rings from her left hand, the gold of her wedding band and the sparkling diamond of her engagement ring.

"My children? Anne and Louise?"

"They're all taken care of."

My mother was making lists in her mind: the meeting next week with the American Nurses Association, how she was supposed to finish that grant but the time had just flown by; which socks to pick out for her girls when they went out to lunch—the ones with the lace on top? Which dresses should they wear? The dotted Swiss dresses she had just made? She needed to brush their hair. Then she couldn't think anymore. The words ran together like slush; there was not even a thread of thought she could hold onto out of the labyrinth of pain. All the neatness of her life exploded.

Dr. Simon, their friend, an expert plastic surgeon, was called. He drove forty miles from Bound Brook Island to the hospital to help my parents. He would drive there every day and monitor their care during the rest of his vacation. He was scheduled to do plastic surgery on the Hiroshima Maidens, twenty-five disfigured women brought from Japan to America for reconstructive surgery, upon his return to work. Later he would set up a hospital in Vietnam and treat victims of the war.

He broke into tears when he saw my parents, he told me many years later. "Your mother had the worst facial burns of anyone who lived, worse than anyone I worked on even after the bomb was dropped on Hiroshima."

In the first forty-eight hours, a burn victim experiences an unremitting loss of fluid and swelling of the burned areas, which sometimes leads to shock and decreased blood flow to vital organs. A full-blown stress response involves urinary excretion of nitrogen and potassium, the very elements of life. Large, non-grafted areas are open to infection. Many burn victims die quickly. My parents were given penicillin, streptomycin, and other antibiotics. Major microorganisms can invade the skin, even from the air. Large areas of dead and dying material are excellent places for bacteria to multiply. First, bacteria can multiply locally, then go to the lymph nodes, and then to the bloodstream, resulting in septicemia. Bacteria can come not only from the patient, but also from dust, blankets, and antibiotic-resistant bacteria in hospitals.

Contact with anything and anyone could have led to the death of my parents, especially my mother, who had been closer to the explosion and had mostly third-degree burns. The degree refers to the depth of the burn. The surface is called the epidermis. The second layer is the dermis, which has hair and sweat glands, nerve endings, and its own blood supply. A first-degree burn affects only the epidermis, the outer layer, while second- and third-degree burns affect both the dermis and the epidermis.

My mother had third-degree burns over her face, neck, and legs. Sometimes the burn is so deep that it goes to the muscle and the bone.

She was continuously given glucose in water intravenously, but her veins were thin and hard to find. Sometimes it took two or three painful pokes before the nurses could get the fluids coursing through her body. The electrolytes needed to be balanced. A sodium solution was also used—just the right amount of salt and sugar, not too much, not too little, in just the right amount of water, but not too much lest it drown out the sugar and salt. It was a balancing act, like life itself. Their bodies needed to be at the right temperature, not too hot, not too cold. My mother hovered near death; only massive amounts of the right fluids, the antibiotics, and the constant cleaning and bandaging of her charred skin gave her a chance to live, to resurrect from the fire.

Dr. Simon cut off the hanging skin from my parents' bodies and clipped my mother's light-brown curls, now smoky and black. The nurse put pressure dressings on their burns, filled the IVs with high-protein fluids, and gave them sedatives. An ophthalmologist friend arrived late in the morning and used a metal rod to pull their eyelids back. He did this twice a day so the burned skin wouldn't stick to their eyes and leave their lids permanently closed or open, rendering them blind.

The word got out fast to the Cape Cod community. You could read about it in the *Cape Cod Standard*: "Dr. Nayer and his wife critically burned. Two small children and a maid not injured." Two of their own—medical professionals—desperately needed their help. A Red Cross nurse, a young woman with a husband and two small children, volunteered for the job. She found babysitters, and told her husband she was needed.

"I'll stay with you all night," she told my mother when she arrived, tending to the burns, and sometimes just sitting next to her and lightly brushing her arm. "I'm here with you, I'm here with you," she'd say when my mother woke up moaning in the middle of the night. Many nurses in the community heard of my parents' plight and pitched in, doing round-the-clock shifts, hour after hour, making sure that they were getting fluids and being turned, and that their bodies weren't ravaged by infection.

My mother and father could do nothing but lie on their beds, wrapped like mummies in white gauze. They had to be bathed, fed, toileted, and turned constantly. In unimaginable pain, they lay there, the hours punctuated only by the ticking of the wall clock, the sound of the sea breeze that had given them such pleasure only the day before, and the movement of nurses and doctors coming in and out of the room. My mother would no longer be able to hold my sister and me in her arms, or brush our hair back from our foreheads before we went to sleep at night, or tell me that the monsters weren't hiding in the wall, waiting to get me. Completely immobilized, she couldn't even ring for help.

The first night in the hospital, only ten steps away from my mother, my father lay in a twilight state. He hated the hum of the machines that he had looked at as a physician only weeks before, measuring the signs of life. He was no longer only weeks before the confident physician walking in and out of the room, always moving, never staying too long in one place, his stethoscope hanging proudly around his neck. Upon his graduation from medical school at Columbia University, his immigrant parents had given him that stethoscope, like a promise. They had worked eighteen-hour days, hoping their children would lead better lives. They read the *Jewish Daily Forward* and believed in working for a better life for all. My father thought he would make his parents proud. He would help people, not just the rich. He had worked for the New York City Fire Department and for a clinic, as well as in his own practice.

"Mama. Mama," he called out softly like the small boy he had been, the boy with so much hope. He could feel his mother with him now in the hospital, a lumbering presence with huge, soulful eyes. She wasn't telling him to come to her, to pass through the tunnel, to leave this life. No, those eyes that he saw were telling him to stay calm through the pain. Those eyes were telling him: You have children, my grandchildren whom I never knew. You have a wife. Finally, before he fell into a deep sleep, he thought he heard his mother say, "I love you, Herm," and felt her wrap him up in her ample arms as if he were an infant, her warm, deep breath syncopating with his own.

When my father woke up, a nurse was checking the IVs, her face masked, her hands gloved. He smelled latex and then something rancid, as if he were already dead. Dead like his brother, mother, and father. This must be death, or worse, he thought. He tried to see a white light when he closed his eyes, something to pull his mind away from the pitch-blackness, punctuated only by the sound of the match being lit, over and over again.

One strike and you're out, he thought. One strike and you're burned all over. He was a failure now. His hands were burned. He might never be able to practice medicine again. His life would amount to nothing. He saw the flames engulfing him and tried to scream, but everything hurt too much, so he only made a slight movement. The nurse, sitting next to him, lifted her head momentarily to look at his vital signs, and then all was still again. He could see everything. He hated the humming sound of the fluorescent lights. For a minute he tried to believe the nurse sitting near him was his wife. Dorothy. Pretty Dorothy. When he remembered that his wife was nearby with a charred face and black, charred hands, he wanted to puke all over himself, over his life. But nothing came up. His children. He could hardly say their names, his Annie and Weezie, so young. He didn't want anyone to come near him, to see him like this.

"I couldn't even kill myself, I was so helpless," he told me years later.

When the sounds of Cape Cod—the low, grief-stricken moaning of the foghorn—began to fade, the morphine drip did its job again, and he descended into the pit of sleep.

My mother was being monitored even more closely than my father: her IVs, fluid intake, output, calories, all the building blocks of life itself that could be toppled so easily, were checked constantly.

"Anne and Louise?" she asked Bernie Simon in a muffled voice. "Anne and Louise?"

"They're fine. Bitten is taking them to the beach. They miss you terribly, though."

My mother tried to turn her bandaged face to Bernie, but she couldn't move a single part of her body as he lightly touched her left shoulder. Her hazel eyes, usually so full of light, looked vacant.

That day Annie, Johnny, and I swam in the bay. Just as the stars had flattened, the water had stopped moving. Annie kept walking toward the water and then back to the sand. She hardly dipped her feet in, even though the day was hot. We both sat under Bitten's umbrella. She kept giving us drinks and trying to get us to eat, but I clutched my stomach and looked at her without saying a word; my insides churned. We just wanted to go home and hear news about our parents. We returned to the house on Bound Brook Island at the same time as Dr. Simon, and we all looked at him expectantly as he put down his black doctor bag, just like our father did every night. Annie and I hoped for good news, that our parents would get out of the hospital soon. Della had said seven days. We sat silently on the long living room couch, arms touching, twinned now, near the spiral stairway that led up to three small bedrooms.

"Your precious parents are in the hospital getting better," he said as cheerfully as possible. "They miss you and love you." Annie and I eyed him like a friend one moment and like a stranger the next. We were too scared to talk or do anything but sit silently with our arms touching, because we knew: it was all over him. The smell of the burns, the antiseptics. The grief.

Chapter Seven

WELLFLEET FIRE DEPARTMENT
ALARM RECORD

Date: July 22, 1954 Time Chief called: 3:30 a.m.

Property Location: Harold Gardner Cottages

Fire Location: In cellar

*How it started: As a result of defective safety valve on
water heater*

Time all out: 4:20 a.m.

Officer in charge: Chief Rose

Officers Responding: Chief Huntley

Chief investigated scene. Closed off gas tank

*Detective Killian notified at 4:30. He arrived at 8 a.m.
Climbed down ladder to the pit, found defective auto-
matic safety valve. Both tanks of gas ordered removed and
Chief needs to inspect before occupancy.*

Picked up red flashlight.

The spiral staircase is what I remember most about the Simons's house. We had to climb it each night, step by step, rung by rung, to get to our bedroom at the far right of the house. Though I knew to be careful, that I could slip easily, I wondered what it would be like to fall down, to get hurt. During that week, Annie would often have her hand on my shoulder, or we would sit next to each other on the couch as if we were twinned souls. The voices of the adults broke apart like molecules. Bitten tried her best to make us feel safe, to tuck us in at night. What she didn't say was what haunted us. We had twin beds, but I always asked Annie if I could sleep next to her, and I did, keeping Baby with me. Bitten never told me to go back to my own bed in the morning when she woke us up. Her eyes were pools of water. At the house, we stared out the window like orphans.

My mother and father waited on gurneys for the ambulance that would take them to the airport. They were going to Beth Israel Hospital in New York City, the hospital where my father had worked after he returned from the war in 1946. They were leaving for an unknown fate—perhaps death, if something went wrong, anything, like a loose IV line that hadn't been checked or an infection, just a tiny red patch of skin left untreated that could lead to septicemia. My father drifted in and out of sleeping and waking, imagining he was with his two girls on the beach, just as he had been a week ago. He wanted to hit something, but he couldn't even pound the sheets because his hands were bandaged. He couldn't cry because the tears would sear his skin with salty water, like the salt water he had bobbed in last week, holding Annie and me one at a time on his shoulders, our arms around his neck as he stood in the knee-deep blue sea and we looked down the sandy strip of beach from our high perch.

"Look, Daddy, a bird! Look, Daddy, a big seashell! Look at the seaweed, Daddy!" He heard voices, one after the other, calling out to him. I was still practically a baby, Anne older now, wanting to know more and more each day. What kinds of questions was she asking now? He shivered. He didn't want us to become like those children that Anna Freud wrote about, Jewish children and others who were separated from their parents during World War II—sent to the country to survive. Living in small country towns, the bombs dropping on the big cities, they imagined the worst and missed their parents so terribly that, later, even those who were reunited with their mothers and fathers were troubled, unable to love, their eyes as blank as stones.

If he strained his neck and looked over toward my mother, he would see the truth: she looked monstrous. How could he have allowed her to bolt ahead, so stupid, stupid, stupid. And she was in terrible pain. She was on a seesaw, he had heard the doctors and nurses say, seesawing between life and death. His Dorothy. His children. Everything he ever wanted! He and Dorothy shouldn't even be alive, he thought to himself, closing his eyes, feeling the hurt and grief wash over his body in waves and seeing himself now as only half human, walking into an infinite blackness. Maybe the plane would crash. The children would be better without them, taken care of by people who weren't burned and half alive.

"The plane is at the airfield," a nurse called out. "Gloria, the nurse, is here to get the patients ready for takeoff."

"Careful," Dr. Simon said. "Let's do this slowly. All the IVs need to be attached. No need to rush."

One by one, the gurneys were loaded onto the ambulance as Dr. Simon did a last check of the IVs and waved good-bye. Perfectly round, cumulus clouds floated thousands of feet above him in a startling blue sky, and high above, the bright, gaseous sun blazed on the blue waters where all the vacationers splashed in the sea.

The ambulance drove on a country highway for fifteen minutes to get to the small airfield at the edge of Hyannis Port, the first time my mother and father had been moved out of their beds in over a week. The car swerved on the narrow, curvy road, bumping over small mounds in the concrete. My mother threw up, and the nurse had to clean her and make sure she didn't aspirate her vomit. For a minute, my mother gazed out the window from under layers of gauze, wretchedly aware of the distance between her and Annie and me. She wasn't sure she would ever see us again. She sank into blackness.

"Damn it. Damn it. Damn it. This is no good. No good. I don't want to go anywhere," my father said as his gurney was loaded into the small plane. The pain was subsiding as the morphine took over, but being moved at all was frightening. How could he survive a ride in a small airplane? How could his wife survive? What was he? Everything closed around him, the plane door locked, the windows shut. Nowhere to go. But the thought of Beth Israel comforted him. All his friends, the familiar hallways.

The husband-and-wife team who flew the plane had over twenty years of experience transporting sick patients from the Cape and other parts of Massachusetts to various places on the Eastern seaboard. Gloria talked my mother and father through what would happen over the next two hours. Even as they drifted in and out of consciousness, she was certain they were aware of her steady voice. They would fly at 25,000 feet. Her husband, John, was a master pilot and a registered nurse as well, and she was also an expert aviator. They would avoid turbulence so as not to disturb them, but sometimes it was unavoidable. My parents were strapped in tightly to their beds. There was no way they would fall. Gloria would be with them the whole time. They had all their fluids attached. They would be met in New York City and taken to Beth Israel Hospital. Everyone would be waiting on the other end: the doctors, the nurses, their medical friends.

"Everything will be okay," Gloria said. "Don't worry. Rest as much as you can. When you wake up, you'll be home." At the word "home," my mother's burned and swollen eyes fluttered for a minute. She looked like she was seeing a ghost, her hollow pupils registering a quick flash of light, as if being called to the other side. But her children were still on this side. The sound of the engine pulled her back and the light vanished. My mother almost died many times during those first few weeks.

The plane rose in the sky on a gorgeous, late-July day, the sun illuminating the small houses of Hyannis Port, the sea so blue, my parents lying still, subliminally aware that they were going farther away from their children. Gloria made sure the IVs stayed attached and prayed that my mother wouldn't vomit again. Cleaning her was difficult—Gloria had to wrap my mother's hands in new gauze and use a rubber suction tube to clean her mouth.

Gloria and her husband had flown out of the Cape many times. They knew the flight pattern well and the airstrip at Idlewild where they would land. New York City Fire Department cars, she was told, would meet the plane and escort the Nayers to Beth Israel.

An hour later, after an uneventful flight, the plane slowly descended to the metropolitan area as Gloria tenaciously held onto my mother's IV stand, which was strapped down but still swayed as the plane dropped altitude. The movement was disquieting to my father, who screamed out in pain and fear and moved from side to side so his bed began to shake. Gloria looked at her watch, read the chart, and decided to give him more morphine. It would be a long ride to the hospital.

"Hold on there, Dr. Nayer," she said.

"Son of a bitch," he said, cursing and crying at the same time. "I can't hold on. There's nothing to hold on to."

The show of support from the New York City Fire Department (FDNY) shocked even the air controllers, who witnessed the engines lumber toward the runway as

the plane landed. My father had worked for the FDNY
for a few years at this point. He would rise in the middle
of the night, get in the fire truck, and be escorted uptown
and downtown, even in hot weather when children had
used up all the water from the fire hydrants and the firemen stood by helplessly, their hoses dry. He was taken
to fires in the winter, his hands icy cold as he listened
for lung problems, bandaged wounds, and sent firemen
to hospitals where he would visit them every day. The
men called our home and my father talked to them, gave
them sick leave, helped them to heal. He felt it was his
duty to do well by these men, and year after year he dem-
onstrated the utmost respect for the FDNY. They took
good care of him, their "doc," and he never lauded his
status over them. So when the FDNY heard about what
happened to my parents, the men were devastated.

Three firemen, dressed in their finest, stood at attention as the medics unloaded the gurneys from the car
and put my parents in an ambulance. One of the cap-
tains, who often worked with my father, had taken time
off to meet the plane. When he saw his doc bandaged,
connected to IVs and moaning softly, and my mother's
burned face and hands, he took his hat off and turned
his face away so no one could see that he was crying. My
father was his favorite medical officer. He had looked forward to asking him about his first vacation with his wife
and two little girls, joking with him as he always did. Just
a few weeks before we left for Cape Cod, my sister had
taken a ride around Peter Cooper Village in the fire truck
and the driver had let her pull the cord that set off the

siren for a minute, and she had laughed with glee.

Two fire engines escorted them through the Midtown Tunnel, where it suddenly got dark. My father opened his eyes, frightened to be underground; he was down the ladder again, in the damp, moldy air, waiting for another explosion. It was a Saturday afternoon, but the traffic was still heavy. Cars slowed down, people rubbernecking, wondering who was inside the ambulance with the two-engine escort being driven through the streets of Manhattan.

When they were wheeled into Beth Israel, at 16th Street and Second Avenue, the humid summer air mixed with the scent of cleaning fluids. My father recognized the pale-green walls and fluorescent lights, the nurses and aides dressed in white, padding fast across the linoleum floors in their sturdy, laced-up shoes. He sighed. They were at home now, in New York, but away from the Cape and all the hope of summer.

For a minute he smelled the salty air of their white cottage. When he closed the windows at night in Wellfleet, his family safely inside, the salt still seeped into everything, into the brown corduroy couch in the living room, into the taste of his lips on his wife's lips at night—those luscious, salty kisses—and even into the newspaper he read in the morning, *The Cape Cod Standard*. Annie had licked her fingers at the beach on the day before they were wrenched from their children. "Daddy. My fingers taste like salt!" And she laughed, small balloons of laughter. Now the beach was still strewn with seashells and the waves still broke across the street, but here he was.

What a joke God had played on him! What had he done wrong? Should he have been more religious and studied the Torah like his grandfather wanted him to do? Why did he deserve this?

He closed his eyes and felt the pain shoot through the burned places on his body. His children were lost to him. At least they were not burned. Thank God, he said to himself over and over. His children were not burned. But he kept hearing their voices calling to him, needing him, and he couldn't stand it. Who would read a book to Anne? Who would check Weezie's tummy when she complained? Who would hold their hands like only he could as they walked into the sea? Who would hold them as safely? What was going to happen to his little girls? What if nobody watched them and they drowned? Who would care about them as much as he and Dorothy did?

A few of his friends, nurses and doctors, spoke in hushed voices to each other and walked a little too slowly to their gurneys as he and my mother were led to the elevator that would take them to their second-floor rooms. Though he opened his burned lids once in a while, he tried never to make eye contact. He couldn't stand the thought of anyone asking what had happened. He wouldn't look at them. Everyone seemed so fake with their fake concern. When he was dead, he wouldn't have to look at them. He was glad his parents were dead. He'd feel too ashamed to see them. They slaved eighteen hours a day to give him a good education and now this! How would he get money to pay all the bills? He'd have to find out about his insurance, his disability. Before the

accident, everything had been in place. He had a bur-
geoning practice; he wasn't sitting around reading the
seven volumes of Proust's *In Search of Lost Time,* like he
had been when he first opened his office after the war,
waiting to hear footsteps on the steep stairs.

"I'm so, so sorry about the accident, Hank," Dr. Post
said, as he rushed by like a ghost on his way to see a
patient. "I'll come and visit tomorrow, after you get settled." My father lifted his head slightly and then tried
to ease into a comfortable position, but everything hurt:
his face, the left ear practically blown off, his neck, his
chest, his hands. Settled, he thought. Yes, they would be
settled here. The account was settled. Their life was settled, settled into horror, failure, stupidity. Suddenly, he
hated my mother. He wanted to blame her for going too
fast, for being so impulsive. "I know what I'm doing,"
she would say emphatically. She was so direct. So certain.
Then he heard her cry out in pain as the elevator button was pushed and they were escorted to their rooms.
Dorothy. He loved her so much. Beautiful, kind, strong
Dorothy. Bossy Dorothy. Efficient Dorothy. Dorothy,
the mother of his children. Why did he let her go down
to that cellar!

My father was taken to the back room and my mother
to the front of the adjoining rooms they would share.
They each had their own bathroom and a separate
entrance, but the way their beds were placed, they could
talk to each other across a small passageway, a narrow
passageway of grief and comfort—my mother waiting for
his words of comfort, my father wanting to die.

Dr. Arthur Barsky would be their chief surgeon. He was skilled, dedicated, and also the head of plastic surgery at Mt. Sinai hospital. Soon, he too, with Dr. Simon, would be working on the Hiroshima Maidens, doing free surgery for twenty-six women, handpicked among so many who had been disfigured by that fiery atomic blast.

Barsky walked into the room coolly, looked at the chart and not directly at my mother's face. "We'll proceed as fast as we can. Debridement and then a number of surgeries. The face first and then the hands." He glanced at my mother for a millisecond. "Get some rest now," he said, and walked out of the room.

"Critical condition," she heard Barsky say outside the door to the nurse, who was just starting a new shift. "I've never seen anyone with facial burns like Mrs. Nayer's who lived." Then she heard his footsteps pad down the hallway. After that first visit, my mother wept.

At first, she was tended to with a flurry of activity. Two physicians checked her fluids while the nurses hovered around, doing this and doing that. So much doing. She was aware of little because of the strong sedatives and the pain, and saw only the shadows of nurses and doctors. She knew she was being cared for, but like someone who had lost a limb, she had lost a part of her that could never be recovered. Part of her was still down in that cellar. The damage. She often said when a bill came, "What is the damage?" smiling flirtatiously at the waiter or clerk. Now she didn't want to know. That pit. That horrible pit.

She pushed the thought far away, glad to be in Beth Israel and quietly aware of the big clock that sat over the bureau. Just like the big school clock she got for her girls to tell time. Anne already knew how to tell time. Soon Louise would learn, too. Louise still did "bunny ears" with her shoes and often asked Della for help. That would have to stop. She needed to talk with Della about that. She didn't want her children to be spoiled, to be dependent on Della for their every whim.

It was now almost 5:00 p.m. in New York City, and the humid day was transforming into a cool evening, the kind of evening when my mother would put on light rouge and dark rose lipstick, her beige linen dress and her lavender shawl. She and my father would go out to dinner at Luchow's on 14th Street, walking the ten blocks. She would loop her arm through his, and sometimes he would put his hand in his pocket. She would have the cinnamon crêpe for dessert. It was so warm and buttery, and big enough to fill a porcelain dinner plate. She knew she shouldn't eat it all by herself, but she knew she would, enjoying every luscious bite. It would be her treat for the week. She could taste the sugar, cinnamon, and warm butter all melted together.

The children could have macaroni and cheese. Not made with too much milk, because Anne didn't like it when it was runny. Our mother would send Della to Gristedes to get vanilla ice cream, whipped cream, and maraschino cherries for dessert. A sundae surprise. She wouldn't tell them except to say they would get a treat. That would make leaving easier, especially for Anne, who always wanted her daddy to read to her. Della should read *A Hole Is to Dig*. Anne could almost read along, and Louise liked the mashed potatoes picture and tried to memorize the words to keep up with Anne.

Drifting in and out of consciousness, she was subtly aware of an IV being attached to her and orange sherbet being forcibly spooned down her throat. It was a spoon with a rubber tip, like the spoon she used to feed us when we were babies. The sherbet was so cold in her mouth. For a moment she remembered playing with her brother in the freezing air of Pennsylvania, putting a carrot on the snowman's face. Her face, she thought. Her face was burned, so close to the match. And her hands. She shivered; her body felt icy cold even though she had three blankets on her. Where was Hank?

"Hank," she cried out, barely audible. "Hank," she cried out again, but the effort of that one word exhausted her, so she started to drift back to sleep. He was so close to her, just in the next room. She could see the edge of his bed and the outline of his body in the sheets. He didn't respond.

She had important meetings coming up at the American Nurses Association—she must get in touch with Shirley. Now she couldn't hold onto anything in her burned hands. Not her husband. Not her children. Not even the notes for the meetings. She could see notes flying into the sky like feathers off a plucked bird. She was a plucked bird, the skin plucked off her, the hair plucked off her head. She remembered the sharp pain of the scissors moving through her scalp, her smoky, burned hair falling on the Hyannis Port hospital floor. Her wedding rings were also gone, removed right away so they wouldn't embed themselves in the blistering skin. They were in a drawer now. Could she ever wear them again? But she was in good hands, even though her own hands were no good right now. No good. No good. She shivered and wanted to pull one of the blankets farther up, but her hands were wrapped and her voice was so faint that the nurse couldn't hear.

Sometimes she thought she was in the Cape Cod Bay with the girls, wearing her pink cotton swimsuit with the shorts that covered her "Bully bottom" (Bully was her mother's maiden name) and slightly-too-fleshy thighs, and a spaghetti-strap top. She always wore a white hat, like a baseball cap with a brim, to keep out the sun because her skin was particularly sensitive. The English and sitting on beaches didn't mix. They ended up looking so silly, like red lobsters, she thought. She never wanted to look like that. She was careful to keep the children covered, too, since Louise had light skin. She was grateful that Anne had a bit more olive, from her dad, so she didn't burn as quickly. She thought of that morning when she had made lemonade from a can, small bits of lemon floating in the water, and roast beef sandwiches with the crusts cut off. Anne liked mayonnaise and Weezie didn't. So much to remember. Sometimes she gave them a sandwich and said, "Don't complain." As a child, she herself had never had so many choices.

Chapter Eight

Each day that went by took me further away from my mother. I forgot the smell of her rose perfume and the feel of her soft lap, where I had sat only six weeks before on Cape Cod—one hand fingering a tiny shell, following the circular road of its body up to a tiny peak, spotted with brown dots like the markings of a newborn fawn, the other hand resting on my mother's knee, my fingers sprawled over the flesh from which I had been born.

"Now, when the plane takes off, make sure to chew your gum," Aunt Peggy said to Annie and me; we each clutched a yellow packet of Wrigley's gum in our hands and walked on the slick linoleum floor through the Boston airport to the gate. We were flying to New York City to pick up our clothes. Then our Uncle Louis, our mother's brother, would come for us. I was happy to taste the sugar coating on the roof of my mouth. I put more and more pieces of gum in my mouth, so it was hard to chew. As the plane rose into the air, I leaned my body against Anne's.

Anne and I sat over the wing, watching the propellers turn, and the static, whining sounds of the engine wrapped around us. When we soared thousands of feet in the air, I looked out the window and saw clouds resembling long-necked dinosaurs, and rabbits with cotton tails like my mother's white cotton balls that sat in the frosty green, antique glass bowl on her makeup table. Della said my parents would come back in seven days, but I had counted all my fingers, and they hadn't come back. Della had left to look for a new family. I missed everyone. I missed the taste of waffles, the smell of Lucky Strikes, the shiny picture books, the lemon pulp mixed with sand. "Baby, it's okay. Mommy and Daddy will come get us soon," I said to my doll, stroking its featureless face.

Then the sky changed, the clouds ran together in an overwhelming grayness, eliminating all traces of blue, and I panicked, realizing that Anne and I were not attached to the ground. Every once in a while in the thick, gray soup, I saw a light straining through, as if a hallway light had been turned on. I stirred Anne from the book she was reading and pointed to the sky. Anne looked out the window with me and we held hands.

"Lean back," Aunt Peggy said, "and chew another piece of gum." Then the wheels touched ground at Idlewild Airport.

"Make sure to hold your suitcases," she instructed, helping us to get our small bags, which our mother had bought at Macy's just a week before the trip. We stood in line to get off the plane, one on either side of our Aunt Peggy.

"Now stay right next to me. The airport is crowded. I don't want anyone to get lost!"

At the word "lost," tears sprang to my eyes. Overwhelmed by all the people, my stomach churned with a sickly feeling.

"My tummy. It hurts, Aunt Peggy!"

"Her stomach always hurts." Anne put her arm around me.

"I'll get you ginger ale as soon as I can." My aunt's voice was tired.

When we heard the voice on the intercom, "Mrs. Luanne, please go to the information booth," I heard, "Louise and Anne, your parents are waiting," and looked achingly at my sister, who seemed to be endlessly searching the crowd.

Later, as the cab sped through New York, I sat in the child's car seat behind the driver, holding my hands together, pushing my fingers against my knuckles and staring numbly out the back window. The gray concrete of the city shocked my senses after sunny Cape Cod. As we drove down 23rd Street, I saw the red-brick buildings of Peter Cooper Village. Aunt Peggy hurried us out of the cab. We were holding our child-sized, gray-and-black tweed suitcases containing our pajamas, toothbrushes, and changes of clothes. We walked fast past the long line of mailboxes, toward the familiar bright-blue elevator. It took us two flights up to our narrow hallway with its eight apartments, the air thick with the smell of spaghetti and meatballs, macaroni and cheese, and roast beef and mashed potatoes.

Bunny Calvert, our mom's friend who had a hoarse voice, no children, and a cat, lived at the far end of the hallway with her elderly parents. Next door to her, Helaine Honig lived with her husband and two daughters. Helaine bought us presents and had an easy laugh. She would sit with our mom looking at shimmering fabrics that they'd make into clothes: doll's clothes, children's clothes, and skirts and dresses for themselves. Next door to Helaine lived Bunny Moran and Nancy, my best friend. Bunny was divorcing, and sometimes she and Nancy's dad yelled at each other in front of 2 Peter Cooper Road while Nancy sat stone-faced on her pink tricycle.

At apartment 2B, a number I had been taught to memorize, Aunt Peggy pulled a key out of her black patent leather purse. We entered our apartment, which was stuffy and humid because the windows hadn't been opened for weeks. We dropped our tweed suitcases by the living room couch and started quickly down the hallway to our back room, passing our parents' bedroom on the left, the door firmly shut.

"Leave me alone!" Anne yelled when I tagged behind her down the beige-carpeted hallway into our bedroom, which was strangely intact, all the toys and games put away in the closet, books neatly stacked on the two bookshelves. A thin layer of dust sat on our matching light-brown dressers. Our twin beds, catty-corner to each other, where our parents read to us and tucked us in each night, were covered with sheets that had been ironed and pressed by Della and topped with light woolen blankets for the summertime. I pressed my face to the window glass, waiting for Mommy and Daddy, while Anne flung herself onto the bed and sobbed.

"I want my mommy and daddy. I want my mommy and daddy! Where are my Mommy and Daddy?"

"They're hurt, Anne. Too hurt to see you now." Aunt Peggy turned her face away, placing her hand over her

leather shoes with the stiff, black bows were still
I left them, neatly placed in a white, two-tiered
ag.

onder when I can send out my invitations. I want
e eight girls instead of six."

o else? Susan and Elizabeth?"

n't Mommy going to make you a pink dress this
Vith a velvet sash? And me a green one?"

i over to my shelf and grabbed my brown Teddy,
I held in my left hand while holding my blue Baby
ight hand, softly rubbing the triangle dolly against
e, up and down like music.

i of us were suddenly quiet. Aunt Peggy hadn't
e word about Cape Cod.

s get going," she said. I could hear my father's
"Up and at 'em," but not his voice. Peggy made
l corners with the sheets as we got dressed.

n we entered the living room still in our pajamas,
Louis, our mother's short and sturdy brother, sat
dge of our father's favorite red-and-black-checked
iir, talking with Uncle Frank. Uncle Louis rose.

s. I'm sorry about your parents. Rusty and I will
od care of you."

od still for a minute, moving nearer to Anne.
Anne looked at Aunt Peggy, who motioned to
go to her uncle. He came to Anne and me, and
d his arms around both of us. He smelled of
Strike cigarettes, which hung on his breath like
on Della's, though he had a different smell, more
e earth. Anne hesitated for a moment, leaned into

heart. I put my hands over my ears and continued to press my face into the glass, so hard it hurt. Everything felt different now, even the air in the apartment.

"It's time for a bath." Aunt Peggy led us to the bathroom. We made soap sodas in the tub, stirring water and soap into small plastic cups like we usually did, pretending they were the egg creams we got on First Avenue. But instead of feeding each other the white froth and giggling, we smeared the soap bubbles on each other.

"You got it in my eyes, Annie." I grabbed a wet washcloth to wipe my eyes.

"You started it. Don't play like you didn't, Weezie. I'm getting out of here."

Anne quickly got out of the tub and grabbed a towel. She shivered. Aunt Peggy bustled in and out of our bedroom, opening our suitcases, bringing our toothbrushes and placing them in the holders on the sink. I lay in the tub for a while longer, looking at the beam in the ceiling and not at Anne. I pulled up the black stopper as hard as I could to see the water and the soap bubbles disappear down the drain until they were almost all gone. When only a few bubbles remained near the drain, I popped them with my index finger.

"Louise! You'll catch cold sitting like that. Come out and I'll dry you off."

When we were both in bed, Aunt Peggy explained to us, "Your Uncle Louis will be here by tomorrow morning. You'll stay with him for a little while, until your parents are better."

Anne usually talked all the time, but she said nothing now, not even to me. Her eyes were hard pebbles. She curled herself up tightly like a snail. Aunt Peggy kissed Anne on the top of her head, brushed her hand across her forehead, and then moved to me. I was counting dots of paint on the ceiling.

"You're going to Sherburne. It's pretty up there. There are lots of trees and grass and they even have a dog." Aunt Peggy brushed my wavy hair back from my forehead, kissed me, and then turned off the light. When she left the room, I held Baby close and lay as still as Anne, my muscles taut. If I am perfectly still, I believed, I can do no damage. I tried to become a tree by putting my arms down at my sides and imagining my hair stuck up like branches. I held my breath and counted to myself. When I finally exhaled, my eyes filled with tears. No one had seen me as a tree.

When an ambulance, the siren blaring, screamed down First Avenue, I clenched my hands into white-knuckled fists. I opened them only when the siren had passed. From one side of the bed to another, I continued to move restlessly. I always had eczema, but tonight the cracks behind my knees itched more than usual, and I scratched them, feeling dots of blood forming small red pinpricks behind the knees on my yellow cotton pajamas. I rested my head in my hands and stayed up for hours, listening to Anne moaning and grinding her teeth as she moved from one position to the next. I gazed around the room like a searchlight. If I stayed up and kept watch, maybe I could bring my parents back. Then I heard a knock on the door and two men's voices. Aunt Peggy was crying.

"They want to see them them?"

"You can't tell them too Aunt Peggy's tall English h "horrible, horrible burns," an time later, when I still cou Louis's voice.

"They might not have en said, his voice cracking. Th into the kitchen to get him

"Time to rise and shine."

Aunt Peggy was bendin good morning kiss. Anne around the room. She w Then she hunched over lik *Charlotte's Web*, the book sh how Charlotte died but her and looked over at Annie, to the window to Annie's tions. I was waiting for my When Anne said nothing, myself and squeezed as har

"In September I'll be se flat line. "Maybe Mommy if she's better."

"I love Schraftts. We replied.

I got up, running my le opened the closet door t

his chest, her eyes brimming with tears that she would not allow to overflow. Uncle Louis lightly touched the top of her head. I buried my face in the round part of his stomach.

"It will be okay." But his voice sounded thin. I looked at the striped curtains on the living room windows, the curtains my mother had sewn, the curtains Aunt Peggy half opened, trying to let in only so much of the world.

We ate breakfast quietly at the small kitchen table, not saying a word, then came back to the living room and stood in front of our uncle like statues.

"Make sure they have mittens, gloves, and hats," Uncle Louis said to Aunt Peggy. "Winter in Sherburne is much colder than here. And they'll be outdoors more."

"How about Baby?" I was alarmed at the word "winter." I held Baby closer to my face.

"Of course you can take Baby," said Aunt Peggy, putting her arms around me.

"I want my mommy and daddy!" Anne cried out.

"I want my mommy and daddy, too!" I said, following Anne's lead and trying to hold her hand. She ran into the bedroom and slammed the door. I slipped into the room and lay across my bed. I couldn't bear to be without my sister. I would do whatever she wanted me to do.

Aunt Peggy knocked on the door. Anne didn't answer, so Aunt Peggy quietly walked in and sat on her bed. Anne scooted over closer to the wall, her face in her pillow.

"Your parents are in the hospital. They're getting better. But they need time to heal. They'll get you as soon as they can."

"Why can't I see them? Or talk to them? You're lying. They're not even alive!" Anne continued to sob until Uncle Louis knocked on the door and came in the room.

"Anne. You need to get ready to go. As soon as your mom and dad can talk to you, they will. Get ready. Aunt Rusty, your cousins and our dog, General, are all waiting for you."

Anne searched through her bookshelf for *Charlotte's Web* and clutched the book to her. She looked at the picture of the spider web on the front cover, tracing it with her fingers. Then she opened the book to the very first page and read out loud between sobs, "To Anne, Love, Daddy." Tears dripped down her cheeks. I was sitting up straight like a rod.

Uncle Louis grabbed our suitcases and we left our house. We left New York City.

Chapter Nine

"Don't put your legs on my side," Anne said angrily as we climbed into our parents' red Dodge, which Uncle Louis had driven back from Cape Cod. I sat far to the right and Anne on the left, sinking into the red plastic seats, torn in a few places from years of wear. The car still smelled of the beach; tiny bits of sand had embedded themselves in the protruding foam. Aunt Peggy opened the door on Anne's side, kissed each of us and told us to be good, as if being good would change anything.

I heard voices in the car, floating like ghosts. Where was my mother? She always held the map and sometimes argued with my father. He might turn the wrong way; she would give him the directions.

Uncle Louis kept talking, his words erasing the hidden sounds as he drove smoothly out of the city. I liked his voice. I wanted to meet my cousins.

"Remember, I get carsick," Anne said.

"You only get carsick when the roads are hilly," Uncle Louis replied.

He drove up the West Side Highway, onto the thruway, out of the cityscape of Manhattan and into the country. The thick, hot air of summer was thinning. Next month, the leaves would turn, bits of yellow flecking the hills.

"You only get carsick when the roads are hilly," Uncle Louis said again, naming the towns: White Plains, Poughkeepsie, and Hudson. After two hours of traveling, Anne and I both drifted in and out of sleep, our faces pressed into the red plastic seatbacks.

"Lunchtime, girls." He opened the car door, and we entered Howard Johnson's restaurant holding hands, the room filled with noisy customers and whirring fans. We ordered hot dogs and milk shakes.

"We have a dog named General who lives at our house. And the farmers have a dog named Shep who is out in the field most of the time chasing grasshoppers in the summer." Our eyes widened: two dogs, grasshoppers, farmers.

"Girls," Uncle Louis called out, after chewing a French fry and taking a sip of his milk shake, "can you believe I used to have an ice cream parlor? It was called Daubert's."

"Where is it? Can we go to it when we get to the country?"

"No. I had to let it go. It didn't work out. But there's an ice cream shop in town. We'll go there sometime. Now eat up, so we can get back on the road."

Louis Daubert, my mother's younger brother, left Staten Island to move to South Forthright, where he and his brother-in-law, Norman, went into partnership on a dairy farm. Later, the farm, cattle, and machinery were auctioned off, one by one. They both lost their life savings. Now, he was selling office supplies and living in one half of a farmhouse, struggling to survive, but there

was no question that he would take us in. When he told
Rusty and his own children about the accident, they all
took a deep breath and spent days preparing a room for
us and making sure that Anne could be enrolled in second grade. Though the world of upstate New York on a
small dairy farm was eons away from the life we had led
in New York City, the Dauberts would love us, feed us,
and teach us to do chores; we would become country
children, running on the rocks, escaping into the woods,
and later ice skating on the nearby pond.

While Uncle Louis was driving us up to the country, so
far from Beth Israel Hospital, my parents had the same
argument through the passageway. My father had wanted
us to stay in New York City with friends, to keep us close.
If we were walking on the cement sidewalks near the hospital windows, so near to him, perhaps he could get a
glimpse of us from the second-floor window. And if he
got out soon, we would come running into his arms. He
would lift us up, high over his head like birds, like he did
when he came home from work at night.

But my mother was firm. She wanted us to stay with
her brother. She knew he and Rusty would take good
care of us. It didn't matter that we were so far away, on
a small farm in a one-stoplight town, and that in a few
months the fields would be covered with snow.

The kitchen workers opened their doors at midnight for
the first two weeks that my mother and father stayed at
Beth Israel. They had known my father for years, had

seen him walking with patients down the long hallways. At Beth Israel Hospital, the staff served him lunch at the cafeteria where he always ate a pastrami sandwich on rye. They liked his kind voice, the way he looked people in the eye. He often joked that he picked this hospital to work in because of the pastrami and rye bread.

Many of the staff who volunteered their time didn't know my father but had heard the gruesome story. Two nurses said they would come in on the weekend and make sure the refrigerator was stocked with the food that he and my mother needed. They took the time out of their summer nights to fill the freezer with orange sherbet and mocha ice cream, day after day, night after night.

"I've got some sherbet," one nurse said. "Can you open your mouth?"

My mother felt the tightness of the gauze around her face, an almost breathless constriction. But she could smell the sherbet, and wanted the coolness to soothe her throat. She opened up slightly, like a featherless baby bird, and the cold substance barely made it into the small opening among the bandages.

On August 6, just fourteen days after the accident, my parents were given anesthesia and wheeled to different operating rooms for the first debridement. Torn and damaged skin must be separated from the body. Applying wet dressings can help the skin separate, similar to the way taking a warm bath will loosen a hangnail so it can be ripped from its source. In my parents' case, so much was being ripped from its source, they were like animals being skinned. The doctors cleaned their burned skin with Phisohex and flushed the areas with a saline solution. This was done carefully, with sterile gloves, a face mask, sterile sheets, and a sterile blanket covering them. The room had been sanitized that morning (the cleaning person had worn a mask), then everything had been taken out, even the cardboard carton that the Phisohex had come in. Germs lived everywhere: on the surface of cardboard, hidden in the crevices of the walls, even in the tiny hairs on the doctors' arms.

The debridement carts were carefully set up, organized in specific kits. A cleaning kit with all the cleaning solutions, numbered, always in the exact order. Then the instrument kit with scalpels, straight scissors with different points, curved scissors, blunt scissors. The instruments were laid out in the instrument tray, always in the same order. The doctor and the nurse had to know exactly what was there; their patients would be asleep for only a prescribed time.

The wet, antibiotic-laden dressings on my mother's face were removed and Dr. Barsky cut away the loose skin with sharp scissors. He opened the blisters with a hook and cut them away as well. As he worked, Barsky saw the depth of the damage: the burns went down to the bone. He cleaned the eyelids, which would be grafted first in the next week. Otherwise, she could go blind from the corneal damage. Her head was shaved again so no microorganisms could nest in her hair, which had turned from light brown to black. The doctor cleaned her face, cutting away dead tissue from her nose, her lips, her cheeks.

Then he cleaned around her neck, carefully clipping off hanging pieces of inflamed, blackened skin, and handing them to the nurse to dispose of. The surgeon moved on to my mother's hands, the scalpel working fast and accurately in his hand. No skin could be hanging off, nothing where infection could fester. My mother's operation took more than an hour.

After the debridement was finished, they applied fine-mesh gauze with light petroleum spirally around all the burned areas, her face, neck, and hands. Then they applied cotton layers with just the right amount of pressure. Not too much pressure or it would have a tourniquet effect and stop the blood supply, but enough pressure that nothing could grow inside, multiply, and kill her. When she left that room, still groggy, she was wrapped up again. Seven days later, she would be given anesthesia again, for the next debridement. There would be no skin grafts until all the dead skin had been cut off, thrown away, disposed of, disappeared.

Just a few doors down, my father was debrided also: all the surfaces cleaned, the dead skin cut off, piece by piece. His burns were mostly second-degree, not third-degree. The hair follicles on his face had prevented the extraordinary damage that my mother suffered. He still had his lips, and his eyelids would shut. They might need grafting, but the grafts would take for sure.

His hands had suffered the most; third-degree burns covered parts of his right hand. They needed to work hard on his hands, so he could return to work. He would have to recover, to see patients again. Thank god he wasn't a surgeon, they thought, when they saw the extent of the damage. Dr. Barsky used the sharp scissors first and then the blunt scissors to make sure all the dead skin was cut away. He worked on both hands for a long time, but especially the right one. The thumb was at an angle, though, from the rest of his hand. My father would need intensive physical therapy to move his fingers.

Then they wrapped him up with pressure dressings and wheeled him back to the room next door to his wife. Soon the nurses would wake them both to feed them. They must keep up their fluids, Dr. Barsky said to the nurses. Of course, the nurses already knew this; they had always been there, sitting at my parents' bedsides, checking their fluids. In seven days, they would have the next debridement. My father would then be ready for grafting, as long as the skin was kept clean and free of infection. For my mother, it might be longer, but not much, as the burns needed to be covered. Slowly, very slowly, the surgeon would replace their burned skin with skin scraped off their stomachs and thighs. The scraped areas would crust over, like the skinned knees of their daughters when they returned from the playground. But their daughters had small, round scrapes on their knees, whereas they had massive, seven-by-seven-inch pieces of flesh—skinned thighs, skinned stomachs, skinned bodies—crusting over, trying to heal.

Every day from now on, my parents would be taken to the tubs of warm water filled with saline. They would each be taken off the gurney and put on a shelf that would be lowered slowly by pulleys into the water. The first time my mother was lowered into the salt water, she cried out in pain. They nurses had to take her out, give her more pain medication, and try again later in the day. The salt solution, though important for cleansing her skin, burned her again; for a moment she had flashes of the original pain and lowered her face into her chest and wept. My father moaned during his first submersion and was also given more medication. Twice a day they would have to endure the baths.

A few hours after their first baths, they were both wheeled back to their rooms, and woke up almost simultaneously.

"I'm thirsty," my father cried out. The nurse got up and gave him a drink of cool water. His hands and face, especially, had begun to hurt, a stinging pain that wouldn't go away.

"More morphine," he said. She picked up his chart, read the instructions again, and gave him some morphine.

At the same moment, in the next room, my mother's nurse was also giving her water and checking her IVs. She added another dose of Percodan when my mother winced upon opening her eyes. My mother heard her husband cry out for water and wanted to talk with him, but she didn't know what to say.

"Hank," she cried out from her room, "Hank, did you get some water?"

He gave the usual monosyllabic response.

This lack of affect, this deep depression that my father had slid into, was the wall my mother had to climb, even as she grasped, bit by bit, the horror of her face and hands. My mother had always been in control, always known how to dot her i's and mind her Ps and Qs. Her slim fingers, her smooth skin, her husband, her children, her sterling career—she had it all, even flaunted it a bit with her single friends, bringing up Hank and her daughters frequently in conversation. She had her cocktail parties, her pigs in a blanket on silver trays, her paintings from the Greenwich Village Art Festival on the wall, her good taste, her confidence. Many people didn't know that she had "pulled herself up" with hardly any help, except some money that her mother had once given her and that she had put away for a rainy day. It had been the middle of the Great Depression, when few people decided to go to school. "To help with your tuition," my grandmother had said, taking out a thick envelope from under the mattress.

Even with so much of her life damaged, even with her children so far away, she was not going to lose everything. All the mirrors had been taken away.

Chapter Ten

Dr. and Mrs. Herman Nayer of New York City,
burned in an explosion Thursday, were reported today
by Cape Cod Hospital to be in critical condition. Cause
of the blast, which occurred at the Indian Neck cottage
where the couple were vacationing with their two young
children and a maid, was given as a defective safety
valve on a hot-water heater. The couple received 2nd-
and 3rd-degree burns of the head and body. Little dam-
age was done to the cottage and the children and maid
were unhurt. Investigating were Detective Lieutenant
George Killian of the State fire marshal's office and
Wellfleet Fire Chief Charles Huntley.

There it was. The evidence from *The Cape Cod Standard*.

I found this article in my mother's green jewelry box, among gold bracelets and tickets to Lincoln Center, when I was a teenager. My mother must have seen it every day when she picked out bracelets or necklaces; she couldn't wear earrings because her earlobes had been blown off in the explosion. I used to gather up the thin paper, nervous that it would tear apart, and hold it tenderly as the words *burned, hospital, explosion* imprinted themselves on my mind. Then I would place it back in the box. Years later, Annie told me she did the same thing.

Helaine, my mother's good friend, said that when she first visited my parents, my mother repeated several times what the fire chief had told them: If they had not tried to light the tank, the automatic action in the morning would have made the whole house blow up. She was so grateful they had taken the brunt, rather than their children.

We arrived in Sherburne, New York, on a Monday in early August. "Where are we? Weezie, stop leaning on me. It hurts."

"Just a few more minutes." My uncle's hands were still steady on the wheel.

Both of us stared out the window. Where were the people and the houses? Only rolling hills and large, rectangular plots spread out in front of us, all fenced in by barbed wire with occasional white farmhouses and their nearby red barns. Cows milled on the green fields, using their tails to flick off the flies that stuck to their hides in the summer. It seemed lonely—all that land with no people, yet so full of grass and leafy trees. I wanted to show my mother and father, to tell them everything about the ride upstate. I couldn't believe how far away we were from New York, how our winter clothes were packed in suitcases, how Peter Cooper Village and Playground Number Two had vanished. I closed my eyes for a minute to stop the pain in my stomach and to try to remember what my parents looked like.

"I don't feel well, Uncle Louis."

"You'll be fine. We're here." The car turned left onto a small, gravel driveway, next to a large, white house that stood before a small barn and a long, wooden chicken house. Off to the left was a big field fenced in by barbed wire, and farther away were gray rocks that led to thick, green woods. The house had two entrances, one near the road and one on the side, by the driveway. My aunt, uncle, and cousins lived on the side closer to the road, while the farmer and his wife occupied the other side, near the barn.

A pretty woman with fiery-red hair, my Aunt Rusty came out the side door, wiping her hands on her red-checked apron. Robert, a long-limbed middle schooler, was followed by Jean, who was only two years older than Annie. She was tall and thin with lots of freckles and long, red braids running neatly down her back.

"How was the ride, girls?" Aunt Rusty looked directly at us and took us by the hands. My stomach hurt less then, and I liked the feel of my aunt's warm hand, still wet from washing dishes. "Dinner will be ready soon. Hope you like hot dogs."

We followed Jean and Rusty into the kitchen, while Robert and Louis carried the suitcases around to the front and straight upstairs to the room Annie and I would share. Then Aunt Rusty gently led us through a dining room and up the steep stairs. The room was so small that the bed and the brown dresser took up all the space, leaving no place for a closet full of clothes and toys and games like the one we had in our room at home. The double bed was covered by a nubby, white spread with two pillows next to each other. I was relieved that Annie would be sleeping next to me.

"I'll help you put your clothes away tomorrow," said Aunt Rusty, standing in the doorway. "Just get out pajamas and your toothbrushes for tonight."

"You can put your toothbrushes next to mine," Jean added, excited, showing us the small bathroom. "Mine is the yellow one."

When I walked down the stairs, the smell of the hot dogs made me sick. I had to use the bathroom and rushed back upstairs. I threw up all my lunch. Brown, smelly liquid coated the edge of the toilet seat and even trickled on my white t-shirt.

"My goodness," Aunt Rusty said, climbing the stairs after me. "Now you need to rest." She wiped off my mouth and shirt with a wet washcloth, felt my forehead, and showed me to the couch downstairs in the living room. Everyone was suddenly silent. I was ashamed to be in a new house and cause so much trouble, but Aunt Rusty kept coming to the couch to sit near me.

Annie came by, too, and sat next to me, our legs touching. She looked out the window, as if searching for something.

Aunt Rusty brought me chicken bouillon mixed with water, so it wasn't too hot. Robert, Jean, and Annie sat at the dining room table across the hall. Uncle Louis carried out hot dogs on a large white dish. On the table Aunt Rusty placed a bowl of red Jell-O with small bits of Del Monte canned fruit floating inside. I heard fragments of conversations as I drifted in and out of sleep.

After dinner, Jean and Robert helped to do the

dishes. "You'll help tomorrow," Aunt Rusty said to Anne. "Weezie, too, when she feels better." We had never helped with the dishes before.

Later, while Jean and Anne played cards in the living room, I got up and walked out to sit on a small wooden chair near my aunt in the kitchen. She had placed the chair there for me, so I could watch her clean up. I swung my legs back and forth because they didn't touch the floor.

"Where's your dog?"

"I think Robert let him in the front door."

I jumped up from my chair to see him. General was a brown-and-white basset hound with big, floppy ears. He was lying in the living room on the braided rug near the heating vent. I petted him on the head, and he twitched and wagged his tail. I watched his tail go back and forth, thumping on the floor. I kept petting him over and over and watching his tail wag until his big, black eyes began to close.

With the twilight fading, Aunt Rusty hung up her apron on a wooden peg near the sink and came into the living room to tell Anne and Jean to finish their card game.

I looked up the stairs toward my new room and grabbed my sister's hand. I was scared of the nighttime. We walked upstairs slowly. The steep stairs didn't curve in a circle like at the Simons's. I wanted General to come up to the room and sleep near me, but Aunt Rusty said he was too dirty.

"Do you want to say your prayers?" Aunt Rusty sat on the edge of the double bed. "Something for your parents who are sick."

"We don't say prayers," Anne said and then bit her lip.

"Okay. Maybe tomorrow." Our aunt leaned toward us, her silky hair falling down her back. "Just pray for your parents. They love you very much."

Anne turned her face to the wall and stiffened up. "They'd come get me if they were alive."

"They're too hurt right now."

"I don't believe my mommy and daddy are alive," Anne said, wrapping her arms around herself and crying. "They'd come for me."

"You need to keep thinking of them. Of course they're alive and they love you!"

Tears dripped down Annie's cheeks. Aunt Rusty sat on our bed for a few more minutes. I said nothing, but I was noticing her red and curly hair. I wanted to touch it, feel it slip through my fingers, but I turned my face away, toward Annie. She was sniffling into her pillow.

"Goodnight, girls," our aunt finally said. "Call if you need anything. We'll just be downstairs."

"Goodnight, girls." Uncle Louis popped his head into our room. "Get a good sleep. See you in the morning."

The next morning, the smell of pancakes and Uncle Louis's voice lured us downstairs. Aunt Rusty squeezed six places at the small kitchen table. I sat next to Annie and across from my cousins.

"Good morning, girls. Breakfast is ready." A white platter full of pancakes sat on the middle of the table.

"Help yourself," Uncle Louis said. I put three small, perfectly rounded pancakes on my plate—everything round, the pancakes, my plate, the plate dotted with small yellow flowers, the clock on the wall.

"You can ask for the maple syrup if you want," said Aunt Rusty.

"Please pass the maple syrup." I was trying to be polite.

After breakfast, Aunt Rusty assigned us jobs. Anne sat up straighter at being asked to do a job she had never done before. She carefully carried each plate to Aunt Rusty, who put them in the soapy water in the sink, sending up millions of soap bubbles. I was afraid to carry the big plates, so I picked up the sticky silverware and put it in with the dishes. Robert and Jean washed and dried the dishes while Aunt Rusty wiped off the table and my chair, where I had spilled some food. I looked up toward the ceiling, pretending I didn't see her cleaning my chair.

Then Uncle Louis walked quickly out the door. I ran to the window and stared at the empty field and at the car turning right and disappearing.

"My stomach hurts, Aunt Rusty." I took the last fork from the table to the kitchen sink. I watched a measuring spoon float for a minute and then drown in the soapy water. A few minutes later, I threw up all my breakfast and lay quietly on the couch again with a cool washcloth over my face.

Anne walked toward me and then away. I knew she wanted to run in the fields with Jean, to get away from me. But she held my hand, even though her eyes would look to me and then to Jean. Her eyes were green and blue and brown mixed together.

"Are you okay, Weezie?"

"No, my stomach hurts." I reached for her hand but she slipped away, toward Jean, who stood at the door waiting.

"You'll be okay. Aunt Rusty is here. I'm only six."

I saw my aunt take the broom out of the tall kitchen closet and sweep the kitchen floor, arranging the white ceramic salt-and-pepper shakers and putting away some dishes in the high cabinet. I lay on the couch for a long time, thinking of my dad's black leather doctor bag.

"What's the matter, Weezie?" he would say, his liquid brown eyes looking directly at me. "Get some rest. You'll feel better tomorrow." Sometimes he would press lightly on my tummy, and I would point to where it hurt. He would tuck me in tightly, feel my forehead, and then kiss me goodnight. My mother would bring me tea and toast on a small, round tray. Later, I'd fall asleep to the sounds of "Peter and the Wolf" on the record player or to the planetary sounds of my parents talking, voices rising and falling like musical notes or like the waves at the beach. When I couldn't sleep, breathing hard from a cold, my throat sore, or my stomach upset, I would listen for Peter's sound, so clear and full of light.

When Anne and Jean returned, a half hour later, I drifted in and out of sleep.

"She'll be fine, Annie. Let's you and I go upstairs and start to unpack," Aunt Rusty suggested. Annie ran upstairs because she wanted to pick the drawers on the left side of the dresser, the ones that she had told me looked a little bigger and were right under the window. For the next half hour, Aunt Rusty and Annie organized our clothes, putting underwear and socks in one drawer and pants and shirts in another. Since the room had no closet, my aunt took the dresses, poplin red-and-white-checked dresses with hats to match, and put them in the downstairs closet. Jean never had dresses like those.

That evening, I got up from the couch and ate dinner with everyone. I sat on a phone book next to my cousin, Robert, who helped me cut up my meat into small pieces. Then I went to my usual spot to pet General while Anne and Jean played cards. I wished I had a friend my age, but Robert always came over and sat next to me.

Before bed, Aunt Rusty held me on her lap and read me a story while Uncle Louis and Robert worked on a model airplane set on the kitchen table. Soon it got dark. I looked out the window of the living room and saw how far the field ran before it disappeared. In the country, without lights, the night was dark like the pupils of my eyes, like ink. I climbed behind Annie to our room. We brushed our teeth and got into bed.

A few minutes later, Uncle Louis came upstairs. Anne was hugging the wall as if it were a doll. My hair had small curls from the humid summer weather. I twirled them in my fingers, remembering how my mother always told me what pretty curls I had. When Uncle Louis bent down to kiss me, I turned toward my sister. He wasn't Daddy.

"Goodnight, Anne and Louise. Sleep well. We'll all have breakfast together tomorrow morning."

Aunt Rusty came up next. She sat on the edge of the bed and said nothing. She stayed for a long time. When she left, the shadows got bigger.

I saw a skeleton dart across the wall as the wind blew through the white curtains. I thought I heard my parents crying and felt their cries in the pit of my stomach. I wondered if they were crying for Annie and me. But Annie said they were dead, and she was smart. Dead people couldn't cry out of their dry, white bones. Dead people couldn't fill a bathrobe. Dead, dead, dead, Annie made a rhyme. Dead, said, bed, read, dead.

If our parents really loved us and were alive, they would have called. If their bodies were just hurt, their voices weren't dead. But the telephone sat on the brown table downstairs and never rang.

Chapter Eleven

After the debridement, my parents received painkillers every few hours. They lay bandaged as they had in the first week on Cape Cod. My mother was weak, suffering from anemia, and under constant watch. My father stared into space, hypnotized by a vast sea of nothingness. He responded to little except offers of more painkillers.

The good news was that the debridement had been a success: the dead skin had been removed. The threat of infection was lower, but around-the-clock care was still necessary. Some visitors came after the operation, relatives and close friends. One of my parents' close friends told her husband that she would have wanted to die, that it would be too gruesome to have to live her life—to face the world—looking like that. "I know I would rather kill myself." Many years later, that same woman killed herself. My father got the call in the middle of the night and pronounced her dead.

The grafting procedures would continue for many months for my father and for five years for my mother, thirty-seven operations in all, thirty-seven trips to the operating room, under the bright lights, under the knife. My parents were both taken to the operating room to cover their burns with skin grafts, thin slices of skin taken from their thighs or from other donor sites. First, the burned areas were sliced off, leaving a smooth, yellow base. Then the grafts were cut with either a long, sharp knife or a razor for smaller chips of flesh. The knives, of course, had to be sterilized for at least thirty minutes. A thin film of Vaseline would be spread on a donor area. The skin would be picked up and stretched flat with a suction retractor, while the doctor cut it with long, even strokes of the knife. The grafts would then be laid out on the recipient area, wet with a saline solution, smoothed flat with the back of a forceps. The grafts needed to go beyond the edges of the defect.

Then came the stitches. First, the skin would be "fixed" with a stitch that went through the graft, through the edges of the skin, and all around the edges. The stitches should be tight but not too tight, to avoid wrinkles, like when mounting wallpaper. Also, and very importantly, blood should not collect underneath the grafted area during suturing. Blood must be removed by brushing the graft with a blunt instrument. Sometimes a saline solution from a syringe would need to be squirted under the grafted area. Pressure dressings would then be applied.

Each time a grafting procedure was done, my parents had to remain immobilized for days and sometimes weeks so the skin would "take." If the take was not complete, areas would need to be cut away or the grafting repeated. Because of the severe burns on my parents' hands, they both went in for grafting only a week after the first debridement. The grafts would be spread over the burned areas to stop the skin from tightening and to further prevent fluid loss and the ever-possible threat of infection. After a period of time, the donor sites—the huge, raw, open scrapes covering their thighs—became even more painful than the burns.

For my father, most of the split-thickness grafts, the thin layers of skin that were spread over his burns, "took" and didn't have to be repeated. However, after each grafting, he was left with shiny, yellow skin and tremendous pain in his thighs, as if he had scraped his whole thigh on concrete or fallen sideways off a motorcycle.

For my mother, her burns were so deep that many of the original grafts had to be repeated, and she lived with one disappointment after another. The initial grafts on her face, burned worse than any other part of her body, were never meant to be permanent. A thin layer of skin could never cover her deep scars. But those grafts prevented loss of body fluids and guarded against infection.

After her initial dressings were removed, she was able to have soft foods, custards, ice cream, and rice cereal (not unlike the soft foods she had fed to her babies a couple of years before). However, weeks later, her facial grafts contracted and tightened so badly that she could hardly open her mouth to eat or even to speak. Both eating and speaking took great effort. She ate bite-sized pieces of cut-up food while longing for a lamb chop and a baked potato. She and the nurses lived with the constant fear that she could choke; pieces of meat might slide down the wrong way and block her air pipes. Years later, we would all listen to her choke at every meal, sounding like she was dying.

*

When Della Duggan called the hospital and was told that my mother could see her, she put on a light-blue shirt-waist dress and a white button-down sweater. She wore the silver cross that her mother had saved for months and handed to her before she boarded the boat for America at the age of seventeen. Della took the wide visitor's elevator at Beth Israel to the second floor. She checked in at the nurse's station and put on a mask and latex gloves that she pulled tightly over her hands. She found the room and quietly opened the door.

"Oh my dear God in heaven," she said when she saw my mother lying still and wounded, wrapped in bandages, and surrounded by the rancid smell of rotting skin. She put her gloved hands over her masked face and wept. She was only nineteen years old. She had seen sick children, even nearly starving children, but she had never seen someone's face burned so badly it looked like charred roast beef, red and brown. She almost vomited.

"Della, I'm going to be okay," my mother said, her voice throaty and hoarse. My mother tried to comfort her.

"The children?"

"The children are fine."

Della moved closer to my mother and sat down on the chair next to her bed, staring at the wall in front of her. Then she remembered the porcelain doll she had bought at the hospital store.

"This is for you," she said. "Should I put it on the table?"

"Thank you, Della. How are you?"

"I was at the YMCA, but I just found another situation. Mrs. Rennison gave me the money for a month if I need it. I know you won't need me now, or for a while," she said, her eyes flooding with tears.

"When we're all better you can come back. We all want that."

"And Dr. Nayer. How is he?"

"Not very well. He's going to be alright with his burns. But he's too upset to see anyone."

"Oh. Give him my blessings. Tell him I pray for him every day. I go to Epiphany Church, and I pray to God for all of you. I light the candles, always four candles, two for you who are so hurt, and two for the children who aren't with you. All the girls from Peter Cooper send their love to you. Please let the children know how much I miss them, and that I pray for them, too."

"Yes, Della. Let us know if you need money. I'm tired." With that, my mother's eyes started to close. A nurse walked in and shuffled Della out of the room.

Della walked dazed to the elevator, went downstairs and out into the humid air of New York. Six blocks later, she entered Epiphany Church and gazed at the stained-glass windows, the purple-and-green biblical scenes, and at the high-vaulted ceilings. Then she walked down the aisle, clutching her queasy stomach, and sat in one of the pews. She looked up at the windows—at Joseph, Mary, and the baby Jesus—and prayed as hard as she could, the holy family so close and so fragile. Then she got up, lit four candles, and said a prayer for each of us: Mrs. Nayer, Dr. Nayer, Anne, and Weezie. She also prayed to

God that sometime soon she would be reunited with the Nayer family.

Della had come to our family when I was only eighteen months old. Before the accident, I had no recollection of life without her. Losing Della so fast was like losing everything; she sang to me, took me with her to church, and even let me bring Baby to Gristedes supermarket. I would hold one hand of my precious doll and she would hold the other as we walked across First Avenue and entered the store, where I would sit in the front of the shopping cart. I have few memories of my mother before the accident, but Della's cigarette breath and her Irish songs are as clear as water.

During the many summery days that were left before the autumn chill, Anne, Robert, Jean, and I played in the fields all morning and all afternoon, except to help with chores and do some reading and writing before dinner. The field in the front of the house stretched to where the cows and bulls milled, protected by barbed wire. Behind the chicken house, gray granite rocks lifted out of the soil. Behind the rocks, woods beckoned with their large maple trees and beds of moss.

I played near the house, sometimes sitting under a white, wooden awning with the farmer's dog, a white sheepdog named Shep. With my arms wrapped around him, I watched the farmer and his wife doing their work. They rarely talked to any of us. Sometimes they were mean to my cousins. When I got tired, I lay down next to Shep and he licked my face with his pink, wet tongue.

When I got bored with Shep, Robert took me on a walk past the chicken house with its awful stench.

Sometimes, when Anne and Jean tired of running far into the woods, we all played by the granite rocks. Robert would look for sticks and small reptiles, and we girls would pretend to be doctors, nurses, mothers, fathers, and teachers. We brought stuffed animals and even small dolls with us for pretend tea parties. Grandma Daubert, my mother's mother, always put the milk in first and said words like "whilst," which we would imitate and then burst out laughing.

I talked to my dolls, at times babbling like a baby and at others talking like an adult. "You must always stay close to Mommy, do you hear? If you run away from her she'll get sick and die." Sometimes my dolls got dirty and I washed them in the kitchen sink. When Jean and Robert had to help Aunt Rusty with special chores, Anne and I sat on the right side of the house, near the silent road and the barbed-wire fence, and fed our dolls pretend food made of flowers. "Here we go. Eat all your dinner. Yes. Daddy and Mommy won't let you get up from the table unless all your food is in your tummy. Your tummy hurts? Oh well, then stop eating but don't tell Mommy."

On Sundays, the family often went on an outing to a nearby lake. Anne knew how to move her arms and legs in the water, but she didn't really know how to swim. That was okay, though, because the lake was shallow for a long way out from the shore

"Stay still," Aunt Rusty said, and snapped a picture first of Anne and then of me, encapsulated in a dreamy, watery world that Sunday, our short, wet hair neatly cut with bangs.

Anne and Jean splashed each other in the cool water under the huge maple trees. I planted my feet near the adults on the muddy bottom and stared at the weeping willow trees for a long time. "Burned bad . . . hospital . . . hands . . . " I heard my aunt and uncle whisper, words that inserted themselves into everything I did—whether it was sleeping, clearing dishes, writing my name, or swimming in the lake.

Though Uncle Louis was away all weekdays at Norwich Pharmaceuticals, his presence permeated the house: from the smell of his red-and-black-checked flannel shirts to the roast beef and Yorkshire pudding he made for Sunday dinner. He had had hard times as a child; his father left the house when he was only six. He searched for him once, but Grandma Daubert said, "You're never coming back to this house if you go looking for your father."

As a teenager, he was a hell-raiser, but a great swimmer who broke a city record in New York. He was also gutsy, the only one who could tease my mother. "I'm never to be called Dot in public," she had always chided him, but this only made the name stick. He was her little brother and, to him, she was Dot or Darty. So what if she had married a doctor and lived in Manhattan? They had still swung on the Salvation Army swings together; she had still eaten tar; and she had still cut her own hair when their mom was out. No, she could never take the Dot out of Dorothy.

Now, almost forty years old, Uncle Louis had settled into family life. Everything he did was for Rusty and the kids, and now for his two nieces who were thriving in the country. Their cheeks were blossoming red like spring flowers from playing outdoors every afternoon, away from their overscheduled lives and the noise and soot of Manhattan.

On weekends at home, Uncle Louis often played penny tricks with Anne and me. Sitting on the front porch of the farmhouse, Anne and I would stop feeding our dolls mashed red-and-yellow flowers when we heard the clink, clink of his pennies. The dolls, overfed, dribbled out pastel-colored petals onto their plump cheeks when the magic began. Uncle Louis took the pennies out of his pocket, put them in his right hand, then put his hands behind his back. He looked unwaveringly at us, then swept his hands toward us, opened his palms, and showed two penniless hands. The trick was over, the pennies gone.

With that, Uncle Louis helped us prop up our dolls as we cleaned their mouths of excess flower food. I remember the colorful, velvety petals of the mashed flowers, how we loved to feed them into our dolls' tiny, stiff mouths. We had become country children, sitting by the side of a road where a car drove by only once every hour. The empty roads, the spreading landscape, and humid summer days, dwarfed us and our small, human lives. On the farm, there were more animals than people, so we learned to be creatures as well as children, to gaze at the cows turning their heads, mooing, chewing grass, to be wary of the bull with its black, shiny coat. We learned the colors of the summer flowers and the total darkness of country nights.

Everything about my parents was fading away, like a bottle set adrift on the ocean with a message inside, something I couldn't get to. I didn't want to care any-more. Caring took too much out of me—it lodged in my body and made me sick—just as it took too much out of my father, who wanted to float away without scars. If my mother hadn't risen from her deathbed, if she hadn't begun to act, our whole family might have dissolved like fluid from an eyedropper, our DNA spreading into a vast sea.

The others were out playing. Aunt Rusty asked me if I wanted to go to kindergarten. I told her I didn't want to go to school. I remembered Bank Street School in New York, which I had already attended for two years, from 9:00 a.m. to 3:00 p.m. daily. I started school when I was two years and ten months old. Our neighbors who lived down the hall commented that it was strange to see such a small child dressed and out the door for all-day school.

In the afternoon, the children slept on thin, blue cots, while the class bunny hopped across the floor, leaving its brown droppings everywhere. "I want them in a school all day. I don't want to pick up cranky children at noon," my mother said one day to a friend as I clung to her skirts.

"What's cranky?" I asked Aunt Rusty.

"Cranky is when you are sleepy and not in a good mood."

"Oh, I must be cranky a lot. Mommy says so."

Maybe that's why she burned herself on the grass. Daddy, too, I thought, but said nothing. On the day my parents disappeared, I probably hadn't taken a nap. Maybe Mommy had asked me to. I was so cranky that my mother left for the evening all dressed up, even her face dressed up with light-red lipstick and a touch of rouge. Her pretty face. Cranky, cranky, that's what I was, cranky. I wondered if Annie was cranky too. But Annie wasn't cranky, just mad sometimes. Cranky. Mad. Sad. I rubbed my eyes so hard my aunt got upset.

"What's wrong with your eyes?"

"I don't want to be cranky anymore." I burst into tears.

"I'm not going anywhere," Aunt Rusty said, holding me in her arms. "When the other kids go to school, we'll spend the whole day together. You can help me with the chores. We can bake cookies. If you're tired, you can lie down."

"Can I lick the beaters like Mommy lets me?"

"Of course. And you can pet General."

I discovered years later that my aunt was not anxious to send me off to school if I needed her so badly. When my cousin Robert had been three, my mother had resolved that her nephew begin the educational process by getting tested at Columbia University's Teachers College, where she had gotten her graduate degree.

"He's very, very bright," her highly educated sister-in-law said to Rusty. "He might be able to start school early."

One morning, Rusty dressed her three-year-old son in the best clothes she could afford, three-quarter-length wool pants and a matching coat and cap. They met my mother at Peter Cooper Village, and she took them both up in a cab to Columbia Teachers College. He sat in the lift-up child's seat and admired his Aunt Dorothy and her mink stole, though he didn't like seeing the mink's small, lifeless eyes. The test took only twenty minutes, but it seemed like forever to three-year-old Robert, who had to sort beads, remember patterns, and listen to instructions from the tester. All he wanted to do was run into his mother's arms, but he knew that his aunt was counting on him to get everything right.

"He's genius level," my mother said to Aunt Rusty after the test. "You should definitely start him in a kindergarten."

A month later, my aunt again dressed Robert in his best clothes, filled a lunch box with a peanut butter and jelly sandwich, a small carton of milk, and two chocolate chip cookies, and sent him to a Catholic school in Staten Island. He cried for his mom for part of each day. If he didn't keep up with the work, the nuns tapped him on his small, plump hand with a ruler. After two months of torture for both mother and son, she picked him up and waited until he was well over five years old to send him back to school.

Aunt Rusty decided to give me the choice of whether to leave her, to go out into the world, when all I really wanted was to follow her around the house, help put the ceramic salt and pepper shakers back into the closet, hear her voice, and make sure she didn't disappear like the water in the bathtub drain.

Chapter Twelve

On the last Sunday in August, Anne and I set eight plates with special cloth napkins, this time for Grandma and Grandpa Daubert. Aunt Rusty was making macaroni salad when the car pulled up the gravel driveway. She washed her hands and rushed to the front door, lightly hugging our grandparents.

My grandma, Fanny Daubert, was a small, stocky sixty-three-year-old woman, her hair slightly graying at the temples. Grandpa, his hair prematurely white, was even taller than Robert. In his white reverend's collar, which he wore often, he looked imposing until he opened his mouth and said the kindest words. He and my grandmother were upset when my mother married a Jewish man, but since their son-in-law was a doctor, within weeks they were calling him to ask about their aches and pains. Years later, they sent him a card for Hanukkah, even though he never celebrated the Jewish holidays, having been raised as a socialist. Once, when we visited my grandparents in Cooperstown, New York, at their senior residence, my father looked at a picture of Jesus that Grandpa had over the bed.

"How do you know he really looks like that?" my dad asked about the blonde-haired, blue-eyed Christian Jesus.

"That's a good question, Hank," my grandfather said. "That's a very good question."

Grandpa Daubert relished his wife's strength. She was a suffragette who believed that women should have something else to do besides domestic chores. When she lived with her first husband near the Salvation Army homes where they both worked as social workers, she would take a day off here or there to go to meetings. Henry Hesse, my biological grandfather, probably did not like being left to keep an eye on his children while my grandmother marched out into the world with her fierce independence.

Grandma kissed us and then turned her face away to try to hide the tears streaming down her cheeks. I tried not to see the tears, but when I hugged her, my cheeks got wet. I felt her breasts against me. "Grandma's little buttercup," she said. Grandpa hugged everyone, then immediately took me on his lap and pulled a butterscotch candy from his pocket. "Grandma and Rusty don't know," he said. "Our secret." I let my face nuzzle into his broad chest. He then quietly handed me three other pieces. "Shh, don't tell." While Grandpa stroked my head, I spent a long time unwrapping the orange candy before I popped it in my mouth. "Mommy likes butterscotch."

"Yes, she does," he said, his voice quiet and steady. "Yes, she does."

Annie and I put flowered china plates on the table, a blue-and-white gravy bowl that poured from both sides, and the centerpiece, Uncle Louis's Yorkshire pudding, just like Grandma Daubert had liked it as a young girl in England. Slowly, roast beef, mashed potatoes, bread, creamed corn, and fruit Jell-O filled the table. Grandpa said grace. He thanked the Lord for the food and prayed for those who were sick. Amen. We all said, Amen.

During the meal, my mother and father were never mentioned. I knew the prayer was about them, because they were sick. They were like a fistful of broken flowers. No one used their names. I smelled the gravy, clutched my stomach, took the napkin off my lap, and pushed myself away from my chosen spot near Grandpa.

Aunt Rusty took me to the couch and covered me with a green cotton blanket. General sat near me on the floor, and for a few minutes I listened to the small clinking sounds and then the chatter around the dinner table. Everyone was talking about the food, the weather, school supplies, our last week at the lake. I wanted to scream until I couldn't scream anymore. Instead, I fell asleep.

Later that night, when I was in bed trying to go to sleep by counting backwards from twenty, I heard my uncle and aunt talking. "She's having another operation. They're out of her blood type again." I stayed up for hours trying to understand the word "type."

The next day began early. As soon as Aunt Rusty called upstairs, Anne leapt out of bed, excited to wear her new, red cotton dress with white stripes along the bodice. I lay in bed glumly, tired from not sleeping much, and moved closer to the wall. I would be all alone that day, except for Aunt Rusty, General, and Shep.

"Do you want braids like Jean's?" Aunt Rusty called up to Anne.

"Oh, yes!" Anne said. From the top of the dresser, Anne picked up two new, royal blue, shiny notebooks, one for math and one for English, and fleshy pink erasers which smelled like dime stores in September, when everything starts again. She rushed downstairs.

"I'll put these white ribbons around your braids, just like Jean's."

I lay still in bed, facing the wall.

"Weezie, time to get up," Aunt Rusty called. "We have a lot of things to do today. I got you two new coloring books! Cinderella and Sleeping Beauty." I bolted out of bed.

Everyone was dressed up, even Robert, who wore dark pants and a crisp white shirt. After breakfast, I watched with Aunt Rusty as Uncle Louis snapped a picture of Robert, Jean, and Anne, her front tooth missing, all of them standing tall in their new outfits, about to go to Sherburne School together. At 8:30 a.m., a yellow-and-black school bus entered the driveway and whisked them all away.

I was home alone with my aunt.

"Little cat," she crooned, "Let's do the dishes first. Here's another dish, and another."

"Found a peanut, found a peanut, found a peanut, Clementine, I was lost and gone forever, oh my darling Clementine," I sang.

My dishtowel was warm and wet from drying, and even though my hands were small, I carefully placed all the dry dishes on the kitchen table so my aunt could put them away in the high cupboard.

"Got a stomachache, got a stomachache, got a stom-achache, Clementine," I continued to sing, "I was lost and gone forever, oh my darling Clementine. Went to the hospital, went to the hospital, oh my darling Clementine, I was lost and gone forever, oh my darling Clementine"

I felt my stomach churn and wondered about the hos-pital, so clean and white, smelling like the inside of my father's black doctor bag. The hospital that had grabbed my mother and father and taken them into its big, square walls, the place where doctors and nurses like my parents worked, the place my parents must have died. When peo-ple go to a hospital, either they come out or they die.

"Here's a towel, Weezie," Aunt Rusty said, handing me a white towel with a picture of a rooster on the front. "Here's a wet dish." She carefully handed me one plate after the next. Now I was an expert dish-dryer; everyone said so. I put each dish on the counter to dry. We began to sing together. Aunt Rusty knew different songs, but I taught her my favorite song, the one I sang over and over, sometimes in the morning, often in the afternoon, and sometimes late at night. The other kids told me to stop, and Annie pleaded with me to please, please, sing a different song.

"Found a peanut, found a peanut, found a peanut, Clementine, I was lost and gone forever, oh my darling Clementine."

Aunt Rusty looked over at me and chimed in as the soapsuds trickled down her apron and the warm water flowed into the sink. The water from the dishes moist-ened my hands; I thought of my blood and looked at the veins in my fingers, blue spider veins shaped like the shadows on the ceiling of my bedroom in Peter Cooper.

"Louise, what are you looking at?" Aunt Rusty was puzzled by the way I glared at my fingers, trying to see through flesh and bone.

"I'm trying to see the blood. I have blood, don't I?"

"We all have blood running through our veins, and our hearts pump blood. That's what keeps us alive."

My mind started wandering, confused about fire, about the color red; once you are on fire, all the blood drains out into the fire. That's what makes it red like the sun at dusk. All the red around me gets confused with the blood and the burns. Robert's red shirt. What had to bleed into that shirt to make it red? Aunt Rusty's red hair. But I needed her, needed her to have blood safely inside her. Now I knew. New York City was out of blood. All the gray and concrete and even the red bricks of Peter Cooper could not bleed blood into my mother and make her alive. Nothing was left of Mommy. I believed that now, believed it in my own veins, veins which I wanted to rip open to see the blood inside because my mother had no blood. I wanted to be like my pretty mother; I wanted to be with my mother. But all of my mother's blood was drained out by the fire.

"Why don't you go out and play, Weezie?" Aunt Rusty said. I opened the screen door and the fresh air smelled of hay and cows and flowers and the chickens in the chicken house. I walked over to where Shep lay in the grass. He was sunning himself under the white, wooden awning. Shep was my best friend now that everyone was at school.

Knowing that I needed him now, he followed me into the field. The cows were inside the barn, so Shep and I had the run of the field. I dodged the piles of manure and the flies while holding my nose.

"Come on, Shep. Let's chase grasshoppers." The grasshoppers jumped high, leaping and leaping across the grassy field. I leapt with them, running and jumping in circles. Shep followed. When I caught grasshoppers, I cupped them in my hands and tried to hold them. They tickled my palm. Most of the time they escaped from my grasp and jumped onto the grass with their black, beady eyes, camouflaging themselves amidst the stalks. Shep played the grasshopper game, too, but never really wanted the slimy, green creatures as much as I did. He jumped and jumped, leaping with me. I was determined to catch another one. I wanted it now. I wanted to hold one and smash it and break it apart. Finally I got one.

"Look, Shep," I screamed. He came over to me sniffing with his wet, black nose, asking to be petted. But I had other things on my mind. Bad things. First I squashed the grasshopper in my hands and felt something snap, like a wishbone breaking, small and fragile. After the first snap, I looked down at my kill and saw that the antennae on the head were moving slightly.

"Still alive," I whispered to Shep. Suddenly overcome by the slightest movement of the dying grasshopper, I pulled its antennae off and then poked my fingers into its beady eyes. The grasshopper was now shattered and strewn like dried grass as pieces of its body dropped into the field. Only a few legs were left in my hands, and I pulled them apart, thin as thread. I made three or four small, green, slimy pieces out of each leg.

Shep was bored. He whined at me to follow him back home, his pink tongue hanging down. He wanted to go to his water bowl and then lie out in the sun underneath the white, wooden awning. I looked at the confetti pieces of dried grasshopper and I was satisfied. It no longer existed. Not even one tiny part of it.

Chapter Thirteen

My father often thought he would never be able to practice medicine again. All his parents' efforts, all that work, eighteen-hour days at the drugstore to pay for his college tuition at Yale. All of it meant nothing. He might as well throw his degrees in the trash. Burn them up. Burn them in the cellar like he's been burned. And all of them dead. Why couldn't he have died instead of his brother—smart, artistic Philip, so happy-go-lucky, so outgoing? Had he died, he wouldn't have to live this nightmare. Why did he go down the ladder? Why did Dorothy light the match? Why did he hold that flashlight like a dope!

In truth, within the first five days at Beth Israel, the doctors and nurses knew that my father would live if his despair didn't kill him. They made certain not to leave medications or plastic bags nearby. They told him my mother was doing fine and recovering, even though everyone secretly cringed at the damage to her face. He saw her wheeled back and forth, her face wrapped in bandages, and wanted to say something to her, but he couldn't find the strength.

Doctors he had worked with every day visited him between rounds, but he showed little interest in anything or anyone. He could tell from their faces that they felt mainly pity and fear: after all, this could have happened to anyone. Even though he hadn't lit the match, he hadn't been able to stop her. Many times he had nightmares of my mother speeding in front of him on a bicycle, devilishly fast, wearing a long, cotton skirt that billowed over the metal bike. He was running toward her, but could never catch up or make her stop or slow down. He woke up drenched in sweat from these nightmares. He played the scene over and over in his mind. He tried to reach over and snatch the match out of her hand, his voice deep and demanding: "Give it to me. Put it away." But he couldn't. He felt helpless and weak, all his power and his knowledge of fires meaningless.

One night, he dreamed that he did take the match from her, yelling, "No! No! No!" When he woke up, for a split second he believed that the accident had never happened. Then he felt his swollen hands, heard the drip, drip, drip of the IV, and smelled the overwhelming scent of antiseptic, which had sunk into all his pores and coated everything: his burned skin, his bed, the sickly green hospital walls, even the fake faces of the doctors when staring at his ruinous existence.

Despite his deep depression, he did get in touch with his friend Henry Wolf at the law offices of Wolf, Popper, Ross, Wolf & Jones. Henry would help him sort things out. Paul Ross was assigned to the case and wrote a letter to Aunt Peggy, sending her papers for power of attorney. She would have access to the bank accounts, the insurance money, and the disability checks from the New York City Fire Department. A number of friends who were able and willing loaned my parents money, which would be repaid with deep gratitude a number of years later. The checks started arriving immediately after they were admitted to Beth Israel.

After this first letter, taking care of the practical details of their finances, the lawsuit would begin against the Gair and Gair gas company of Massachusetts. If they did not survive their burns, their children might have a chance of receiving a settlement for the accident. My father wanted to make sure of that. The investigation by Detective Killian from Massachusetts showed that there was a faulty valve. The manufacturer would be to blame as well as the gas companies. No additive had been used, so there was no odor, no warning, just an invisible leak into the air. Paul Ross would ask for a lot of money. He was talking about a quarter of a million dollars, more money than my parents could ever imagine.

Even with the movement of the case and the realization that he might survive, my father grew increasingly despondent and anxious, as worries burrowed into every crevice of his brain, making it hard for him to rest. Even if he survived, would he be able to make money again? The deep burns on his hands made it hard for him to move his fingers at all. As a doctor, he knew how badly his hands were burned, how the metal instruments were used to prevent his fingers from growing together. Even with all the splints and bandages, would his hands ever heal? How would he hold a tongue depressor in a patient's mouth? How would he tap the stethoscope to warm it up? What would the patients think about his burned-off eyebrows, his half-missing right ear? How would he touch his wife's body? Would he even want to touch her anymore?

My mother spoke through the passageway when she heard my father moan. "Others recover," she said. Her voice sounded like she had swallowed molasses. "Don't think about the bad things. Think of the children and of me. Don't be so selfish. Work on getting better."

From her bed, between the twilight time when the painkillers put her into a restless sleep and the short time she was awake, my mother spoke again to my father through the small passageway between their two rooms—the space like a breath, but the only bridge they had to each other.

"Hank. Are you there?"

"Yes, Dorothy, I'm here," he said. To her overflowing relief, he sounded a bit like the man who adored her. Then he said, "I just don't know what's going to happen."

It was her turn to remain silent. Would he still love her "through sickness and in health," as they had promised each other in their wedding vows? That's what marriage is all about, she thought, shivering when she thought of her own mother, who had been abandoned by her father and left nearly penniless. Her father's departure had been so sudden. There had only been her mother's screams after reading the note on the dining room table. Thank God the Salvation Army had continued to provide for them and her mother had been able to earn a salary by working in the homeless shelter. The secondhand clothes were sometimes torn, but she sewed them well. Her mother saved up to get her the lace-up boots that my mother wore until the brown leather would no longer stretch to accommodate her growing feet. She always looked good, with her long, blonde curls and the perfect posture that she learned by carrying books on her head for an hour each day, walking back and forth across the living room, her eyes focused ahead. If you stood tall, she often said, people thought better of you.

She and Hank, though, they would stay together. Theirs was a romantic wartime courtship: the quick wedding before he went overseas, the years she waited for him during the war, the pride she felt in marrying him. They loved each other and shared interests and friends. They were parents. They were still young and had so many more years together. She looked at her burned hands and wondered, if only fleetingly, how she could ever go out in the world again. She tried not to think of her face. She knew she wouldn't let her husband leave her.

After that, she began repeating to him: "We can get through this and pick up the children." She would repeat this sometimes four or five times a day: before breakfast, during lunch, in the afternoon when he woke up from his drug-induced nap, and in the evening, the hardest time of all—when the hospital was dark, any sudden noises spelling emergency, the crash carts and then an ominous silence.

"The operation is next week. We'll call the children before then. We'll get to hear their voices."

"I don't know," he would say. "I just don't know what's going to happen."

"Stop thinking about the future. No one knows the

future. Think of now. You're recovering. I'm recovering. The children are well cared for, but they need to come home as soon as we can get them."

Sometimes my father slipped away from her. So she used her voice, which had come back and was strong now. Her voice could help him through. It had to. The children were waiting. Yes, they might be adjusting at the farm, but they were not home where they should be. At the end of the string of thoughts, my mother was overcome with pain, fatigue, and helplessness, alleviated only by the flow of visitors who came to see her: friends from Peter Cooper, Helaine, Bunny, colleagues from the American Nurses Association, Shirley, and all the others, medical friends from the hospital, and family members who were so devastated when they saw her that they couldn't stay long, sometimes vomiting in the hallway because they couldn't make it to the bathroom. She could hear them heave right outside her door.

The worst was her mother, who just sobbed and sobbed in the straight-back hospital chair next to her bed and couldn't be consoled. "It's okay, mom," she repeated over and over. "It's okay." My grandma took a deep breath, gathered all the strength of her Christian faith, put her palms together and prayed to God that my mother would look just like she did before and that her suffering would soon be over. My mother closed her eyes then. She wanted her mother nearby, but she didn't want to think much about God or even be prayed for. Years later, my grandma handed me a touched-up picture of my mother at seventeen years old—with her milk-and-cream complexion and pretty face. I stuffed it in a drawer because I didn't want my mother to know that I had it. "She is my only daughter," my grandma said when she handed me the framed photo in a small, brown shopping bag.

In September, my mother's eyelids were operated on. They had to be grafted so her lids would close as much as possible. Otherwise, her eyes would never shut, particularly the right eye, and she could become blind or sustain corneal damage. The operation was delicate and frightening, and it took a long time. After she was wheeled back to her hospital room, she lived for the next two weeks in complete darkness, terrified that she might not be heard or get the care she needed. Although she could still hear the shuffle of feet and the sound of people coming in and out of her room, some of them didn't talk to her. They replaced soap in the bathroom, cleaned the toilet, and moved trays in and out while she whirled inside a terrifying, dark vortex. Because she was so scared, a round-the-clock nurse was hired to sit next to her, touching her to tell her she was there, reading her letters, letting colleagues visit, and monitoring her every heartbeat. When the bandages were finally removed from her eyes, she felt an enormous relief at seeing the light from the window and the faces of the nurses, doctors, and orderlies who just a week before had been merely disembodied sounds and voices.

The round-the-clock nurse was let go. Instead, the hospital engineer created a footboard for my mother, who was still bedridden with a bandaged face and swollen legs. When she was thirsty, needed pain medication, or just wanted some human contact, she would tap her foot against the board and a bell would ring for the nurse. A nurse would come in with a cool glass of water and a soothing word. Then my mother would fall back to sleep. Sometimes she thought of Rusty—and not herself—putting her children to bed at night.

Ordinarily, in late September, Anne and I would have walked to the edge of Peter Cooper, met the crossing guard, and walked hand in hand across 20th Street and then First Avenue to P.S. 40. I would have been in kindergarten, and Anne in second grade. The autumn air would have been crisp with new beginnings. Anne's birthday was September 24. But it had already gone by. My mother had missed Annie's seventh birthday.

Peggy Rennison, who worked tirelessly to help my parents, sent Paul Ross, who was handling the legal aspects of their case, pictures of my mother and father before their burns: photos taken right after they were married. My mother's light-brown hair was neatly curled around her cheeks and face, and her eyebrows were beautifully arched over her light-brown eyes. She had a striking intelligence and loveliness about her. Gazing into the camera, she looked peaceful, proud of her white silk blouse with a ruffled neck, her small, thin hands simply manicured with light polish, her wedding ring clearly visible. My father's picture was similarly striking. In his handsome captain's uniform, medical epaulets on his jacket, a U.S Army insignia on his hat, he looked directly at the camera. He had a Clark Gable mustache over full lips and strong eyebrows over big, heavy-lidded eyes.

These pictures, before and after the accident, would be the most important evidence in the file.

"Some loose ends need to be tied up and then we will be all set for the institution of action," Paul Ross wrote in his letter to my father. "I hope we can get the post-accident photos as soon as possible." The letter was sent to Dr. Nayer, Room 705, Beth Israel Hospital, where my father would live for many, many months. At least something had been put into action.

On the farm in early October, Robert held my hand and Jean and Anne walked ahead. "Look what I found!" Annie shrieked, running around in circles. "It's like a mirror."

"That's mica," Robert and Jean said in unison. "Mica," Robert said, "is delicate and breaks very easily." He put a glistening sliver in his hand, and Annie and I saw him break it into many pieces. His hand was filled with stars.

"Let's find more," I said. We chipped off pieces of mica, enough to make a small mirror if the fragile pieces could be put together like a puzzle.

"I can almost see my eye in this piece." I held a small sliver near my eye.

"Get that away from your eye, Weezie," Annie said. "You could go blind. You wouldn't be able to see. Everything would be dark." I quickly let the sliver drop to the ground. Annie pulled me toward her.

"I've got an idea," Annie said. "Let's bury the mica under the dirt. In the spring, we'll try and find it. Only the four of us will know where the treasure is buried. We can't tell anyone. Promise, Weezie?"

"I promise."

Just before it got dark, we each dug a hole in the earth. My nails got dirty, even under the skin. We placed the bits of mica inside the holes. Everything shimmered down below. The minerals sparkled inside the dirt. Perhaps the mica would grow, I thought. The sky and clouds could look at themselves in the underground looking glass. We raced back from our adventure, everything about us covered in dirt.

"Where have you all been? Wash your hands!" We all scurried to help Aunt Rusty.

That night in bed, I thought of the hidden treasure and wondered whether it would be there when spring came, or if the earth would absorb it all and make it vanish. Either way, we would try to dig up the mica stars with our hands, after all the snow had melted. We had promised each other.

In mid-October, almost three months since the accident, when Stella Chess, my father's colleague and friend, pushed the elevator button at Beth Israel Hospital and got off on the third floor, she had some idea of what she could expect. As a psychiatrist, she of all people knew how to brace herself for this; she knew what physical and mental suffering was attached to such profound injury. She had heard the gory details. But nothing could really prepare her or anyone else for the reality of my mother's face and hands and my father's burns and despair. There was the smell of burned flesh mingled with sanitized cleaning fluids and the antiseptic swabbed constantly over the burns to prevent infections. What was most frightening and glaring for visitors was that my mother had no lips, only a small hole surrounded by bandages from which, in the first few days of her stay, she haltingly blew out words, sound by sound. Of course she couldn't write, so communication was hard, especially when she had been sedated, which was often, to numb the pain.

My parents believed this meeting with Dr. Chess was critical; their relationship with their daughters depended on it. They had so many questions. How would they preserve the relationship from these sanitized hospital beds and through such a long absence? What should they do? When should they call? How much should the children be told? At what time during their procedures should the children see them?

Dr. Chess girded herself after the initial shock and sat down in the chair next to my mother's bed. She could see in her eyes a vulnerability rarely revealed. Dorothy Nayer was the kind of woman who would say, "If you're having trouble potty training your children, just put them on the pot and close the door. What's the big deal?" She was confident, overly critical, and of decidedly English stock with little room for weakness. Her determination still shone through her words.

"I want them to have a normal life," my mother said, not asking, but demanding that it all be made right. "They are with relatives and getting good care. I don't want this to change too much." Dr. Chess, having studied the effect of separation on children, knew the impact, the rift that grew exponentially each day a child, especially a young child, was deprived of a mother and father, especially two parents at once, so suddenly and without warning.

"We'll make this right," said Stella. My mother's eyes brightened as she reached out her left hand, completely bandaged, but the hand that hurt less. Stella lightly brushed the middle of her arm.

"Consistency is the best," she said. "Calling at the same time each week. The call will be expected; therefore, it will be less difficult for them than if the phone just rang at any time. Also, when Hank goes home from the hospital and when you go home, between operations, don't let the children know you are at Peter Cooper. That would upset them too much, to know you are there without them.

"Good-bye for now, Dorothy. I'll keep in close touch about the children. I'll also write everything down and leave it on the table. They'll get through this and so will you." Then Stella went next door to see my father. She repeated what she had told my mother, but he refused to look her in the eyes; they had known each other for years, respected each other as colleagues, started their families and their practices at nearly the same time. She saw how my father stared at the lime-green wall in front of him and at his bandaged hands, his doctor's hands. She wondered if he would ever be able to practice again. That would be a tragedy, she thought.

"Thanks, Stella, for everything," he said. "I'm tired now. Dorothy will fill me in."

He closed his eyes and kept moving his severely burned hands, wrapped in bandages, trying to get comfortable. All he wanted was another painkiller.

*

"Halloween is just a week away," Aunt Rusty said. "We'll take you to the store tomorrow and get your Halloween costume."

"What can I be?"

"You'll get something nice. Don't worry."

That night, Annie and I started saying our made-up prayer. Aunt Rusty taught us to sit up straight and put our palms together as if they were reaching for the sky. She also said that our parents could hear us praying for them.

"God bless Mommy and make her better soon. God bless Daddy. God bless everyone. God bless the whole world." We continued to say that prayer every night for all the months we were at the farm. When we returned to New York City, we continued to say that prayer for years.

As I drifted off to sleep, I was a ballerina with a tutu made out of lace netting that looked like the honeycomb my mother ate each morning with her Thomas' English Muffin. With the tutu I wore white tights dotted with tiny pink hearts and a pink satin ribbon that Della curled around my high ponytail.

"What are you thinking about?" Anne asked, moving closer to me on the bed.

"About our Halloween costumes with Mommy and Daddy."

I wished Mommy and Daddy could see us in the new ones. But I didn't know what they could see anymore. They must be dead, I thought. The word "dead" sounded as dark as the earth underneath the grass. It scared me. Annie yawned. Sometimes letters arrived on thin, blue paper with notes from "Mommy and Daddy," but Annie studied the handwriting and let me know that it was not our mother's handwriting. It curved too far to the right. She kept saying that it didn't match.

Our bed had two thick wool blankets, but at times we shivered and moved near each other, sometimes clasping hands.

Chapter Fourteen

"When can I see myself in the mirror?" my mother asked one of her nurses.

"It's not yet time." She had been living in the confines of her room for months and all the mirrors were gone. Absolutely No Mirrors for This Patient, the sign read in black ink on the outside of the door and in all the files.

"When can I see myself in the mirror?" she asked again.

"Not yet, Mrs. Nayer," one of the doctors said. "But soon."

"When can I see myself in the mirror?" she asked an orderly, half hoping that he would just let her take a look because he didn't know the rules for each patient.

"Not yet time, Mrs. Nayer." Outside, the trees were beginning to shed their leaves.

"When will it be time?" she asked her doctor the next day.

"It will soon be time," he said, "but not quite yet." She wondered how many operations it would take for them to say it's time, but she didn't ask.

She had an occupational therapy appointment at 9:30 a.m. Frank, a new orderly, picked her up. She was dressed in a red woolen A-line skirt that Peggy had brought from Peter Cooper, and a light-blue, long-sleeved cotton shirt that was too big for her, especially now that she had lost a considerable amount of weight. However, she needed clothes that would fit loosely around the neck, where she had extensive burns and bandages.

By the way people looked at her, moving their eyes from side to side, or turning their heads away, looking at the space around her but not at her, she knew. Her face was no longer pretty. But the plastic surgeons had promised a lot. Even though the first grafts didn't take, the second ones did. The scars were covered now. With makeup she would look good, even pretty again. She would learn more about makeup, go to the counters at Lord & Taylor and have one of the salesgirls give her a lesson. It might be a pain, buying so much foundation and matching it correctly, but it would be an adventure. She would look good. She and Hank were recovering.

The walk to the occupational therapy center took a long time, especially since her legs were spindly from loss of muscle tone. Sometimes she asked to stop in the middle of the hallway to catch her breath. She leaned her 115-pound body against Frank's for a minute. "I need a little time," she said. For the first two months, she had been in a wheelchair, aware of peoples' stares. Now she was walking and dressed in decent clothes. So much progress, each step a move nearer to her old life, that life she had worked so hard for: professional work, a husband and two daughters, friends. Her legs hadn't been badly burned. Only her thighs had large patches where donor sites were used. Her calves were sleek and shapely like a model's. She would buy nice shoes with buckles and bows and soft Italian leather, Ferragamo shoes (on sale, of course) that everyone would admire. That's where they would look, not at her face but at her shoes. Oh, but that was a silly thought. Her face would be fine to look at.

The doctors had told her she was out of the woods. She hadn't gotten an infection. Her lungs were okay. "You're going to make it," they all said, sometimes writing in their charts instead of looking directly at her when they gave her the good news.

My father had also begun to perk up. One day, a man whose hands had been burned came to talk with him. The doctors and nurses had tried many times to get him to talk with burn survivors, but he had always waved them away.

"I don't want to talk about it," he would say, tensing his lips and jaw. They would leave him alone then. Dr. Simon had finally gotten through to my father, though. His patient was allowed into the inner chambers. It was a first.

Dennis Segal, dressed in whites, had his tennis racket with him and looked happy, even though his shiny, yellowed, scarred hands had been covered with skin grafts. The young man opened and closed his fists, showing all the mobility he had gained in such a short time. Instead of saying, "Please go away," or "I don't feel like talking," my father asked him questions: "Were they second- or third-degree burns? How many times a week did you go to therapy? Do you have the same amount of feeling? How about when it gets cold outside? Do you have constant pain?"

Then they started talking about Eisenhower; as they were both Democrats, they hoped someone might defeat him in the next election. Both avid readers, they talked about literature, especially Hemingway's Pulitzer Prize-winning *The Old Man and the Sea*. "What a story," my father said. "Such a solitary struggle that symbolizes so much."

Overhearing the conversation, my mother breathed a sigh of relief. He was coming back to the world. She walked into the women's restroom, feeling more confident that if she ran into anyone, she looked put together in her morning outfit and was now walking on her own, not scrunched up like an old lady in a wheelchair. The restroom smelled of antiseptic, just like her hospital room, but it had a fresh, soapy smell as well. Hospital personnel and family members used this restroom, too. She was slowly moving back into the world beyond her room. She found herself alone with the two porcelain sinks and the three stalls. She noticed that the black-and-white-checked tiling on the floor looked new. Handsomely done, she thought. Unusually nice for a hospital. It was something she might like to have someday in her own bathroom. It still hurt to turn around and flush the toilet—the skin on her neck, face, and hands pulled so tightly—but she did it with greater ease than only a week ago. She smoothed her shirt and rearranged her skirt, feeling so happy to be out in a reasonably nice outfit. She left the stall and went to the sink, picked up the bar of Ivory soap and washed her hands well, lathering between the fingers. Her right hand was curved inward, like a claw, and the warm water still burned in a few areas where the skin was healing. Instinctively, she looked up, and was shocked to see a mirror in front of her.

The anguish she felt when the horribly scarred face stared back at her was quickly hidden, but her stomach churned mercilessly. She took a deep breath so as not to vomit. What she saw was a glimpse of what she had become: her peachy skin replaced by ropy scars, like thick snakes weaving in and out of her cheeks and neck, and the thin piece of skin that supposedly had covered her scars was nothing more than a piece of cellophane; everything showed underneath. It was all so transparent. The doctors were lying. She didn't look better. She had no eyebrows, one eye was bigger than the other, and her eyelids were shrunken. Worst of all, her mouth was a sunken hole, a gash in a sea of scars. She had no lips at all, and the burns that scarred the upper part of her face ran all the way down her neck. Now she knew: what was on her hands was also on her face. There was no difference. It was only worse because her hands could be hidden, placed on her lap or in a pocket, but her face was what she showed to the world; her face was everything.

She left the bathroom in silence and said nothing to the orderly. She walked more slowly than usual. He asked her to speed up a little, please, if she could; he had to pick up another patient. She walked into the physical therapy room and took a seat in front of a basin of warm water. She knew what to do: put her hands in the water and move her fingers. Open and close. Open and close. Open and close. She knew she had more mobility than she did last week, but today she felt defeated. No one would know why. Hank must know—she shivered thinking of how many times he had traced her face with his hands. "So pretty. I'm a lucky man."

A few weeks later, my mother had her first pedicle. She didn't need a mirror to know what that looked like. The pedicle was like a thick, doughy mass of sausage that went from one part of her body to another. First, the doctors collected the skin from her stomach and connected it to her wrist. After the pedicle became viable, meaning her blood began to circulate through it, she underwent another operation. The pedicle would be moved from her wrist to her shoulder, and then again from her shoulder to her face.

After each operation, she had to keep her arm in one place for weeks at a time. Her arm was in a sling but her shoulder hurt terribly. She had to take painkillers not only for the pain of the grafting sites and the surgeries, but also for the muscle strain of keeping her arm in the air as if she were half bird and half human. She longed to put her arm down, to let gravity do its work, but if she moved too much, or made a wrong move, the whole process would have to begin again, and again. The skin would turn blue first and then black. It would happen many times and she would have to start over. These were "the delays," as the doctors called them. One surgical procedure followed another about every two weeks. She was put under the knife, under anesthesia, and each treatment required a long recovery.

This time, she desperately wanted the operation to be a success because every setback took her further away from her children. She needed to have that skin spread across her face for her children. She had to look good for them. She knew she would. It would just take a little more time. She would have to be patient. The grotesque image of her scarred face was just that: an image that she decided to forget. She would think of the future and not dwell on the past. What good did it do to dwell on the past?

Chapter Fifteen

Twelve weeks had gone by for Anne and me without hearing our parents' voices. New voices and images attached to us like the skin that was being grafted onto our parents. When I tried to remember the past, the faces of my mother and father blurred, and the voices that we had heard every day of our lives began to live underwater like sonar.

Long ago, now in the "Once upon a time" realm, on the trip to Cape Cod, Anne and I fell asleep to our parents' nighttime voices, punctuated by "Turn here . . . No, not this way." And then their plans for the next day: "We'll take the children to the beach. The rooms of the house are small but adequate. Della will make the beds once we get there and help with the shopping tomorrow. Are their books easy to find?" *Peter Rabbit, Winnie the Pooh, Charlotte's Web.* "Is Weezie's Baby with her in the back seat? Did Annie's favorite sweatshirt get packed?"

Then came the shock of losing those familiar, comforting voices after they disappeared into the white hospital walls where we were never allowed to go. First, Dr. and Mrs. Simon opened their house to us just after the accident, taking Anne and me to the beach with their son, Johnny. Bitten Simon tried not to reveal the horror by talking in soft, soothing tones. Dr. Simon's voice was cheerful and firm, but stretched out as if he were trying too hard. Then came Aunt Peggy at Peter Cooper with her good-night kisses that replaced our mother's night-time rituals. Now what we heard every day were the firm and steady voice of Uncle Louis, the solid, loving voice of Aunt Rusty, and the happy voices of our cousins, so welcoming. In the past, we had heard their voices only once or twice a year. Now they were everyday voices.

There were no pictures of our parents to help us remember, nothing we could carry in a pocket or put near the bed. No tape recordings to remind us of the old sounds. Everything from the past was garbled and unsteady. First the lines of our parents' faces dissolved. Then their voices changed and flowed into each other.

How could two scared little girls sort through all the sounds to find the two voices of their parents? Would they finally call? When would they call? And if they did call, how could Anne and I believe that the voices coming through the phone receiver truly existed? How could the sounds truly be our mother and father? We had been left so suddenly and for so long. How could our mother and father, so enormously hurt, make us believe that they still loved us, that they wanted us back?

It was the evening of the first phone call from our parents. It was mid-October, and darkness had already descended. The Peter Cooper trees were beginning to shed leaves, the brown sparrows now less visible than in the summer, when they hopped from branch to branch. My mother and father had been released to Peter Cooper for a short time between operations. A practical nurse in a starched white dress and oxfords was hired for round-the-clock care. She and Peggy Rennison were in the house, along with my mother, her hands wrapped in gauze, and my father, who lay on his bed and stared at the heavy, black phone next to his reading light. There were to be no interruptions. Besides the buzzing of the big clock in the kitchen, the house was eerily quiet, the shades drawn, and the children's room in the back empty, a constant reminder of what my parents were losing.

They had thought this through with the help of Dr. Chess. Though Anne was articulate, precocious really, I sometimes mumbled and didn't project clearly. It might be hard to hear our voices filtered through the black coils of the telephone line. The butterflies in my mother's stomach fluttered, as excitable and full of light as her children. She took a deep breath and anticipated Anne cataloging all her adventures, down to the minutest details, in a rush of syllables. Then I would talk about the dogs, perhaps, or my most recent stomachache. Then I might say, "I miss you, Mommy, more than anything." Anne would say that too, yes, how much she missed her Mommy and Daddy. My mother would let our voices wash over her burned body like the balm of Gilead.

It was time. She looked at the bright-white clock, its numbers bold and clear, easy for a child to read. She was sitting down at the kitchen table where we usually ate with Della, where I always asked for a "squishy egg" in the morning. Her children, her babies. It was 5:29 p.m. She tried to relax. My parents had decided that they would call us at 5:30 every Saturday evening. In a minute, the nurse would hold the phone to her ear since her hands, which had just been grafted again, were wrapped in bandages. Meanwhile, in the bedroom, my father was staring at the clock with a mixture of joy and dread. He would pick up the phone in his left hand, the one that had already been grafted a couple of weeks ago. His right hand, which had undergone one operation after the next, was still wrapped in gauze. What would he say to his children? Would they talk to him? He looked at the trees and noted how much they had changed since the summer. How could the seasons change without his children near him?

My mother had it all planned. First, my father would speak with Anne, who would talk about all her activities. Then my mother would speak with Anne, and then I would come on the line. Stella had warned them that the children might be scared, that they might not talk much. Not talk? Inwardly, my mother was annoyed at the suggestion. She expected her children would want to talk with them. *They* were their parents, not Louis and Rusty.

My father had the number written on a piece of lined paper that Peggy had given him. He had gazed at that number almost every day, carrying the crumpled piece of paper back and forth from the hospital to the apartment. His children had turned into this, a flattened line of numbers, remote, detached from him, just like the skin that had been painfully debrided off his burned hands, falling away, layer by layer.

When the clock struck 5:30, he dialed with his left hand. Louis answered the phone.

"Hi, Hank. I hope you're doing better. I've got good news! Louise is finally writing her name. Her whole name. Anne is doing great in school. You should see all her gold stars. And they know how to get the chicken eggs in the morning. I hope the operation went well. I'm going to tell the children you're on the phone."

While Uncle Louis was on the phone, Anne was working on her vocabulary words while I kept writing my name again and again on a pad, finally putting the "e" at the end of "Louis" and not getting laughed at for spelling a boy's name. It had taken me hours and hours of practice, but my uncle and aunt insisted that I be able to write my name.

"Anne, please come over here," Uncle Louis said.

"I'm still doing my words," she said.

"You need to stop because your father wants to speak with you."

Anne's eyes, which had just been completely focused on her words for the day ("sunshine," "window," "door"), now flooded with emotion.

She grabbed the telephone. "Hi, is this my daddy?" A pause, then: "You're not my daddy! You're not my daddy!" she screamed into the phone. "My daddy doesn't sound like that. He's never sounded like that. My daddy doesn't cry. You can't be my real daddy. My real daddy would come and get me and take me home." She dropped the receiver so it dangled for a moment, almost pulling the whole phone off the brown table. She then ran up the stairs to her bedroom and sobbed.

I began shaking and covered my ears with my hands like I had the night after the accident. I wouldn't take the phone, even when Uncle Louis said my mother wanted to talk to me.

"Please, Louise, it's your mommy. She wants to say hello."

"I don't want to," I said quietly and then felt ashamed. But Anne had said it wasn't Daddy, so I wouldn't talk. My stomach hurt and tears sprang into my eyes. I wanted to crawl into bed and stay as still as a tree.

"Dorothy," Uncle Louis said. "Weezie won't come to the phone. She's upset because Anne is upset. It'll be better next week. Oh Dot," he said, his voice softening to his only sibling. "It'll be better. They're okay and you'll get better."

"Bye, Louis," she said, trying not to let him know her voice was cracking and her heart breaking.

Louis tried to engage my father in a conversation, but there was silence.

In Peter Cooper, my father lay back down on his bed and stared at the picture of his two little girls on the bureau in front of him. Clutching a pillow with his left hand, he tried to make a fist, but he couldn't because one hand felt like a tight glove had sucked all the lifeblood out of his fingers and his other hand was wrapped up in layers upon layers of gauze.

"Damn it to hell!" he said so loudly that my mother could hear him cursing from the kitchen where she sat, while the practical nurse put down the receiver.

Peggy Rennison used a Kleenex to wipe off a few tears that had formed at the corners of my mother's swollen eyes. My mother immediately asked Peggy to bring her the Sears catalog from the living room and had her flip to the children's section. Her eyes were drawn to the red, wide-wale corduroy jumpers with matching white turtleneck shirts. Good for the cold winter in Sherburne, she thought, and also smart-looking. She asked Peggy to send the girls the handsome jumpers. "Please send them off as soon as you can. I want them to have the jumpers by next week."

Then the nurse put a patch over the eye that would no longer close and my mother went back into the bedroom, dark now because my father had turned off the light. He was groaning in his sleep. She had another operation coming up and needed rest. Disturbed by Anne's sobbing and my silence, she asked the nurse for more pain medication. She had to rest. She didn't have time to ruminate like my father did.

After the phone call, I stayed downstairs on the living room floor, the lift-up pad by my side. I was paralyzed by the silence. Aunt Rusty tried to get me to finish coloring Snow White, trying to stay inside the lines, but I could hardly hold the crayon because my hands were shaking. When Anne fell apart, all the molecules that held me together disintegrated. After ten minutes, Anne came slowly down the stairs, her shoulders hunched, wiping her eyes with the Kleenex that Aunt Rusty had brought up to her moments before. Without looking at anyone, she walked over to where she had left her homework, sat

down on the couch, and concentrated on her words, saying little for the rest of the night, even when Jean tried
to get her to play Old Maid.

"Could that have been Daddy on the phone, and
Mommy?" I asked Annie.

"It doesn't matter anymore. Just go to sleep." Annie
leaned closer to the wall.

The next morning, she climbed out of bed early, finished her vocabulary word sheet, and went off to play
with Jean in the field. But at dinner that night, Annie ate
little, moving the mashed potatoes and corn from one
side of the plate to the other. She didn't even want to
play with Jean after she finished all her homework.

I stayed close to my aunt all day, so close that I almost
tripped her a few times. I didn't hear my parents' voices,
but I thought I could see them, like thick patches of air
that I flew away from. Aunt Rusty told me to go outside.
I found Shep and put my arms around him; he sat still as
I quietly rubbed his fur. Then I came back inside, sat on
the couch, and stared out the window.

The next Saturday at 5:30 the phone rang. When Anne
had finally settled down after sobbing the week before,
Aunt Rusty and Uncle Louis told both of us that our
parents would call every week at the same time. So when
the telephone rang, it was as if a scream had sounded
from another world. Uncle Louis picked up the phone
and gestured to Anne, who came quickly, her eyes determined, almost rabid, wanting so much to believe this
time that it might really be Daddy.

In Peter Cooper, my mother and father were again in separate rooms. They were determined that the call would be better this time. My father must have used every imaginable trick in his mind to stop himself from crying when he heard his daughter's voice.

"How are you, Anne? Did you have a good Halloween?" he asked, this time a bit of our old father peeking through.

"Yes, Daddy," Anne said, tears streaming down her face. "I was a bunny rabbit and Weezie was a cat. Where are you? Why can't you get us?"

"Your mother wants to talk with you."

"Hi, peachy pie," my mother said, her voice thick but steady. "How are you?"

"I'm okay, Mommy. We got candy bags for Halloween and I'm singing at my school. I'm singing in front of everyone. They picked me and I'm practicing. I also got five pieces of red licorice. Where are you?"

"I'm in the hospital, getting better. Can you put Weezie on?"

I had been staring fixedly at Anne the whole time, wanting to grab the phone, to hear the voices at the other end. When Annie gestured for me to come forward, I bolted from the couch to the phone and Anne put the receiver next to my ear.

"Is that you, Weezie?" my mother said, her voice shaky.

"Yes, Mommy. Where are you?" I suddenly felt weak in my knees; I wanted my mother so badly that for a moment I couldn't breathe. I could smell the sweetness of her voice.

"I'm in the hospital, getting better. I hear there is a dog in the house. Do you like the dog?"

"His name is General and I pet him every day. There is also Shep. He sits with me. I'm scared at night. I miss you, Mommy. Where's Daddy?"

"Daddy is resting right now, but he'll talk with you next Saturday. Be a good girl and listen to your aunt and uncle."

My aunt gently took the phone from me. Anne and I moved trance-like to the couch, our eyes glazed, not talking to each other or to Robert and Jean, but sitting side by side, our arms stiff, our lips shut tight. I was trying to see my parents, to find them in the middle of the room, to connect the voices to something, even to a gauzy ghost that flew in and out of the window.

In the middle of the night, I woke Anne up.

"Go back to sleep, Weezie," she said, but I sat up in bed for what seemed like forever, looking at the shadows on the ceiling, counting up to fifty and back down to one, again and again, until the numbers took over . . . *one, two, three, four* . . . such easy, predictable patterns.

In the next room, my aunt and uncle were talking.

"It was better," I heard Aunt Rusty say to Uncle Louis.

"A lot better. At least they talked. Dorothy and Hank must feel so much better."

"They're adjusting here, Louis. They seem to fit in. It's like they've been with us for years."

"I know."

"They were so quiet after the phone call. So scared. They don't really understand. How can they? . . . We're doing a good job, aren't we, Louis?"

"Yes, Rusty. They seem happy. They're not as spoiled or as sick all the time and they're learning to do chores."

"Louise doesn't put out her shoe for me to tie anymore, like she used to do with Della. Can you imagine one of our kids doing that!"

When I heard their light switch off, I tried to sleep.

Chapter Sixteen

My mother was a letter writer. She wrote letters to her mother every week, letters to friends in England, letters to those who had lost loved ones or become sick, letters to those who had had babies or gotten married. She wrote thank-you notes when others did not. She wrote detailed letters about new wallpaper, new boots, what she had for dinner, museum exhibitions and plays that she and my father had seen. She wrote letters about her job, the state of nursing, the state of the world, letters about her children, their progress, their personalities, their interests.

For years and years, wherever my sister and I went—as we moved from apartment to apartment in our twenties; hitchhiked through Europe in the 60s; experimented with drugs; lived "hand to mouth," as she would say; went from boyfriend to boyfriend, job to job; or ended up in small towns in Canada or in villages in the south of France—her letters always followed us, annoyed us, and perhaps grounded us. That unique script, that tremendous need to put everything in writing: the books she read, the grilled-cheese sandwiches that she had at night but must stop eating because she had put on weight, or something about my father—his practice, his fire department service.

Once, I found a letter she wrote when she was nine years old. In perfect script, she described the new boots that her mother had gotten her: the soft leather, the laces, the buttons, the shade of brown.

So when my mother's right hand was deemed no longer "useful," she spent hours trying to write with her left hand. One nurse brought her a wide pen, so my mother could grasp it better and write the letters more clearly.

"Dear Annie and Weezie," she started over and over. She would almost get to "How are you?" when she would have to stop. Her hand hurt. She hated using her left hand. It wouldn't work. Letters would not form correctly. Sometimes, when she was alone on her hospital bed, so as not to show anyone her frustration, a few silent tears would fall on the page and smudge the ink. She would throw her pen down and take a nap. When she awakened, she would again pick up the pen in her left hand and try to form some letters, any letters, an A, a B, a C, but they came out all wrong. She had, before, written so quickly, so skillfully. Now she couldn't even write one word that anyone could read. She had to dictate her thoughts to the nurse.

As her hopes of ever being able to use her right hand again began to fade, all her dreams of sewing new dresses for her children and a new wardrobe for herself began to vanish as well. Anne and I already had a small doll's suitcase filled with her creations— red and blue corduroy coats with collars and buttons, dresses made of black-and-yellow flowered fabric with tiny snaps, just the right size for the Madame Alexander dolls she had gotten us when we were three and five. She had bought us the small, plaid suitcase, where we kept the doll coats and dresses on tiny, white plastic hangers.

She already had plans to sew organdy dresses for our birthdays this year. She had bought the patterns and was going to shop for the fabric in September. Now Anne's birthday had passed. Her own daughter's birthday, another year of her short life. But she tried to push those thoughts away.

My fifth birthday came on November 22. "Happy birthday to you, Happy birthday to you, Happy birthday dear Weezie, Happy birthday to you," everyone sang as I came down the stairway for breakfast.

That day, I helped my aunt sweep up the breakfast crumbs, dust the bookshelf, and make my bed. I worked on my letters in the afternoon until dinner. We had my favorite meal, macaroni and cheese. For dessert, Aunt Rusty brought out a vanilla cake with vanilla icing and I blew out the candles as everyone sang again. I opened two boxes sent from my mother and father from the hospital, one with a thick red sweater with shiny brass buttons; another box had two board games and three Peter Rabbit books. I opened one of the books and saw the shiny pictures. For a minute I could hear my mother's voice reading to me at night at Peter Cooper and in the lazy afternoons of Cape Cod.

Aunt Rusty, Uncle Louis, Robert, and Jean gave me a doll I wanted. She wore a white sleeper and came with a plastic bottle that you could fill with water. After "feeding" her, you could take off her clothes and watch her pee. Aunt Rusty got mad because she found little puddles of water on the floor and on the couch, so eventually I put her away or made sure to put a washcloth under her bottom before letting her pee. Annie made a card for me at school, a multicolored tissue-paper flower with the message: "To my one and only sister. Happy Birthday, Love your sister, Annie."

By the time I turned five, I had been in Sherburne for more than three months. I stopped clutching my stomach and lying on the couch. I became a country girl, among the fields, cows, dogs, and chickens. I was becoming my aunt and uncle's child. When my mother and father called me the Saturday after my birthday, I told them about my cake and thanked them for the presents they sent me, but all I wanted was to play with the doll my aunt and uncle bought me, the doll that could pee when you gave her a bottle.

Thanksgiving came a few days after my birthday.

"Weezie, Anne. After breakfast you'll help set the table," Aunt Rusty called up from the bottom of the stairs, her right arm resting on the banister as we brushed our teeth. "And Grandma and Grandpa will be here in the afternoon."

"Can I put the tablecloth on the table?" Anne asked.

"I don't see why not," Rusty said as she descended to the kitchen and put out bowls of cereal. Jean and Robert were already eating and had a lot of chores that morning while Uncle Louis drove to pick up Grandma and Grandpa Daubert.

Four hours later, the table was set, even more beautifully than on Sundays, with lace napkins and a new platter where the turkey sat. Grandpa said grace.

"God in heaven, we give thanks for all your bounty on this special day and send our prayers to those who are injured or in need of thy care. We give thanks to you, Lord in heaven. Amen."

"Amen," everyone whispered.

Thank you. Amen, I repeated inside my head, tasting the words as I let Grandpa fill my plate with mashed potatoes, stuffing, turkey, and gravy.

After dinner, I went over to the couch and sat on Grandpa's lap and held out a book for him to read, the Peter Rabbit story where he slips under the fence and past the evil Mr. McGregor.

"What does injured mean, Grandpa?"

"Injured means hurt," he said.

"Are Mommy and Daddy still hurt?"

"Yes. We must keep praying and never let up."

I was quiet for a minute. I didn't want to keep praying. Part of me just wanted to give up, not to think about the voices that never became my parents. I didn't want to think about the writing that Annie said was not my mother's or about the father who was not my father. I didn't want to think at all. At night, sometimes I dreamed of a big, black umbrella, a huge umbrella that would block out all the other thoughts, a totally inky sky on which nothing could be written. Nothing. No letters. No thoughts.

Since my father was not burned as badly as my mother, between his grafting procedures, he would go home to Peter Cooper and often fret about the court case and the lack of income. He knew he couldn't go back to work for a very long time, so he obsessively read and reread the letters sent to him by the lawyer.

Dear Dr. Nayer:

I just received the original complaint prepared by Gair and Gair. One signature is enough—it's not necessary for Dorothy to sign. I call your attention to two things: First, you will notice that the complaint is only against the Gas Company and does not include Sears Roebuck and the manufacturers of the valve in the heating unit. Gair and Gair are of the opinion that the case against them is not too strong and therefore do not want to jeopardize the possibility of a substantial recovery against the Gas Company by the defendants blaming each other, as a result of which your claims may suffer [. . .] In addition there is a cause of action which seeks $50,000 for you as a result of the injuries sustained by your wife. In law, when a husband is deprived of the consortium of his wife through the fault of another he may recover damages for such loss.

I do hope that you are both getting along well. I still have not received the post-injury photographs which I hope will come in due time.

Sincerely,
Paul Ross

He began to despair. They couldn't prove the gauge was faulty? So what case did they have? The additive in the gas was not, as he understood, federally mandated.

Maybe they would have no case at all. Maybe he couldn't ever go back to work. Maybe it would be better if he just died, he thought.

When he sat in the living room and stared out the window, watching the rain or snow fall gracefully on the empty branches of the trees, he relived the moment of the accident: the lit match, one small match unleashing all the horror, the flash of searing fire, climbing up the ladder with his flaming clothes, he and Dorothy rolling in the grass, the frightening plane ride to New York, not being able to talk with his children for so long, to explain anything. He felt like a deflated balloon. Life was flat, devoid of sound.

He was mired in the past. As things began to improve and he realized he would live, he understood that this meant he would have to face more surgeries, his wife's face, his children who had been lost to him; he would have to face the world. So as he got physically better, his mood plummeted even further.

Chapter Seventeen

On the farm, November came and went quickly, its freezing temperatures often hovering around minus forty degrees, the kind of cold that freezes your blood so that frostbite might appear like little white snowflakes, capillaries spreading out in intricate patterns. On the weekends, Anne, Jean, Robert, and I walked out the door to the vast, white field and made snow forts. We all worked together, sometimes for hours in the freezing cold, diligently constructing a house with an opening for a door and enough room for all of us to sit in a circle, our bottoms icy on the fort floor as we put our mittened hands over our faces to protect our noses and cheeks from frostbite. The wet wool of the mittens had a particular smell in the freezing air, wet and delicate at the same time. One fort we made stayed up for almost three weeks, its perfectly rounded walls thickened with ice from the chilly nights. Nothing melted in those arctic temperatures.

During the day while the others were at school, I gazed out the window at the fort, the pride of our hands, a private hiding place where no adults were admitted. The stark whiteness of the snow dazzled me for a minute, sparkled and shone with prisms of light that poured through the ice like sunlight poured into summer waters.

On Saturday mornings, Uncle Louis and Robert fetched two sleds from the basement and we spent hours going up and down the one hill right next to the chicken house. Robert often took me on a ride with him, our combined weight pulling the sled fast down the cracked and icy snow. When Anne asked to go that fast, Robert took her on the sled too, and Jean and I went down together, sometimes singing or yelling, always bracing for a fall. We tumbled again and again and always picked ourselves up, our hair, cheeks, and even the tips of our eyelids covered with snow.

On those snowy Saturdays, Aunt Rusty had to call us in for lunch two or three times. When we finally came through the door, our clothes dripping wet, our cheeks red, she pointed to a corner of the yellow linoleum kitchen floor. There, we took off our scarves and mittens, which were covered with snow that would slowly turn to mush, thin lines of water snaking across the floor. Aunt Rusty would come by with a mop, and by the afternoon, our clothes would be dry, and we'd race out the door again to play for one or two more hours before dinner.

At night, after drying the dishes, I could hardly keep my eyes open. I would brush my teeth, trudge up the stairs to my bedroom, and wait for Aunt Rusty and Uncle Louis to say goodnight. Annie and I said our prayers. Contented, my whole body tired from hours of going up and down the snow-covered hill, I fell into a deep sleep, dreaming of the next day: skating at the nearby pond, coming home for soup, bread, and hot chocolate filled with tiny marshmallows. After the first two weeks of skating, Uncle Louis no longer had to hold my hand on the ice. I whizzed around the pond trying to catch up with Annie and rarely fell. Sometimes the four of us held hands, like a line of dancers. I thought of Central Park, where Anne and I skated on a huge rink in the middle of New York City, surrounded by tall buildings, with my mother and father holding my hands and sometimes picking me up so I flew in the air like a feathered bird.

When Monday came, I missed my cousins and Annie. I looked longingly at the empty fort out the window, wishing I could rush through the opening into the icy room, but I didn't want to brave the elements alone. The snow looked desolate then. Aunt Rusty was busy doing laundry, making grocery lists, washing the kitchen floor, dusting the bookshelves, putting away breakfast dishes, and using the carpet sweeper to get the dust off the living room floor. She went down on her hands and knees and scrubbed for a long time to remove the bits of food caked onto the linoleum floor. Every once in a while, she would stop her scrubbing, come over to where I was sitting, and ask to see what I was drawing.

I was still in the habit of singing "Found a Peanut," "Row, Row, Row Your Boat," and "Three Blind Mice" over and over again. If Aunt Rusty was inside the bathroom, finishing her meticulous job of cleaning the mirrors, she would say, "Again. Sing that song again, Louise. You have such a good voice." I would start up, "Three blind mice, Three blind mice, See how they run, See how they run," repeating verses, adding verses, improvising the tunes until I had almost written a new song. I included General in a verse, his big, brown eyes, his floppy ears. I would also sing about Shep, sitting under the white awning with him and chasing grasshoppers, just the two of us. Shep was my favorite creature of all.

"Shep and me, Shep and me," I sang. "Shep and me and General, too."

I longed to go out, but the cold was brittle and the snow as high as me. Shep was inside the farmer's house, staying warm, so I rarely saw him that winter. I wanted to go knock on their door, but I was afraid I might drown in the drifts that piled up against the white house.

Every morning, Uncle Louis would get up early just after the sun came up, and he and Robert would shovel the snow near the door frame, but by midday the snow had stacked up high again. The others would leave for school. I did the usual chores with Aunt Rusty or sat on the green couch waiting for the other kids to come home. Sometimes I looked at the readers my aunt and uncle had gotten Anne and repeated the rhyming words, "sat, bat, mat, fat," again and again, or drew in my coloring books. Every once in a while, Aunt Rusty would guide me to draw inside the lines.

As the weeks went by, Aunt Rusty and Uncle Louis put more pressure on me to learn my words and to color neatly. I had to be exact. They insisted that I write my name twenty-five times a day on the pull-up pad. Lately, I had gotten frustrated with the task and kept lifting up the plastic before I finished my name. My letters looked crooked, not neat like my sister's. I just wanted to run in the fields that were now covered in snow.

"When are they coming?" I asked Aunt Rusty every fifteen minutes after lunch.

"It's going to be a while, Weezie. Another two hours. Look at some books while I finish the chores."

Two hours seemed like forever. I went up the stairs to my room and came back down, looking for something. When I felt particularly lonely, I spent most of the afternoon lying on the living room floor by the heating vent next to General, who rarely ventured out anymore. I even rested my head on his back and sometimes fell asleep.

"Louise," Aunt Rusty said one day in early November, after we had both put away the breakfast dishes. "Do you want to go to school?"

"Yes, I'd like to go to school. I want to ride on the bus, next to Annie."

That afternoon, while I rested upstairs, waiting for the kids to return, I heard Aunt Rusty dial a number on the phone. As she talked, I knew.

"Yes. Okay. Next Monday? Should I bring her in for an hour or two? I don't need to. Okay." Then I heard some whispering about my mother and father.

As I sat on my bed, thinking about the next Monday, I remembered Bank Street School: the bearded doctor who looked at my throat with a tongue depressor each morning and made me gag; the roof area where I played, and where one day Annie fell and had to have stitches in her chin; the rabbit who hopped among the blue cots during nap time. I wanted to get up and touch him and pet him, but I had to stay in my cot. How I hated having to take a nap. How sometimes Della picked me up and I didn't see my mom until the late afternoon.

"You can come down now," Aunt Rusty called out from the kitchen. She was staring at the Halloween photograph of all of us in our costumes, I in my black cat outfit and whiskers.

"You're going to school next Monday. That's in four days."

I quickly took in the scenery of the house, Aunt Rusty's red-checked apron, the way her hands smelled after she washed the dishes in the foamy water, her long, red hair that I loved to touch at night, the clear and loving sound of her voice, a sunflower sound.

"I'll need pencils and erasers," I said, suddenly panicking.

"You don't need pencils and erasers for kindergarten. There's a slide and swing inside the room. You'll eat lunch there and take a nap. You'll ride with all the others, both ways."

Aunt Rusty then went into the kitchen to put away the dishes.

"Help me with these, will you, Weezie?" she said, taking the clean breakfast dishes out of the rack and putting them on the table. I moved next to her and helped her take the juice glasses from the rack. By now I knew what to do. When all the clean, dry dishes were stacked on the table, I put away the cups in the cupboard that was catty corner to the sink. I could open the doors myself and neatly line up the juice glasses, all the green ones so close they touched, and the clear glasses together, separate but near the others. Next I took the small breakfast plates and put them on the shelf below the glasses. I made sure the middles all lined up, just like my aunt told me to, so if someone grabbed a plate, the stack would not fall down and crash. "We don't have money to replace things," Aunt Rusty said. "We need to be careful with what we have."

That morning, I did my chores without complaining, aware of Aunt Rusty's eyes on me. When I sneezed, Aunt Rusty, who usually told me to go get a Kleenex, got one for me. "Okay, little one," she said. "Now blow your nose. I think we're finished!"

All afternoon, I gazed at the clock, wishing I could tell time. When I heard the bus pull up the driveway, I ran to the door and opened it. I saw Anne come off first, yawning, then Jean and Robert, who were talking to each other.

"I'm going to school next week!" I yelled to all three of them as they walked into the door.

"That's great, Weezie," Annie said. Then she dumped her book bag on the couch, pulled out her reading and math book, and started her homework.

Only Robert sat with me and told me about the school. He described how it looked on the outside. "Like a perfect little house." He told me there was a swing and slide in the middle of the room, and many children to play with.

When Annie and I said our prayers—"God bless Mommy and make her better soon. God bless Daddy.

God bless everyone. God bless the whole world"—they sounded hollow. Make her better soon. Soon had come and gone. My parents had turned into ghosts, thin, tall figures that swept in and out of a narrow passageway. Every time they came close to me and I reached for them, they were sucked back into the tunnel, and I was too afraid to follow. I wanted to tell them that something important was about to happen, but they were not there, and when I did think I saw them, they were without faces and voices.

That night, I woke up to the sound of my aunt and uncle talking. "The grafts didn't take on Dorothy," Uncle Louis said. "That means more time until they're able to get the girls."

"I hope the next operation goes better for her. Poor thing. It's been one horrible thing after the next. And Hank doesn't seem to be interested in much."

After that, their voices became muted as they went into their bedroom. "Not interested in much." What could that mean? That our mother and father weren't interested in us anymore? What does "interested in" mean, anyway? I suddenly felt very cold, and moved my body closer to my sister's.

On Monday morning, I brushed my hair while counting to fifty, put on a denim jumper that my mother sent from the hospital, a blue turtleneck, red tights, and snow boots. I ate little at breakfast.

"You'll be running around a lot. You need to eat something," Aunt Rusty said.

The smell of pancakes, which only yesterday had me

rushing down the stairs to the breakfast table, now made me sick.

After breakfast, I boarded the bus, aware of how steep the stairs were. Robert followed behind and helped me up by placing his hands on my back and giving me a gentle push. I counted eight steps up to the top, making sure to look down so I wouldn't see all the strange children. Suddenly, I was surrounded by children I didn't know. Jean and Anne, who usually sat together, looked at each other. Aunt Rusty had told Anne that she had to ride with me. Anne sat on the aisle and Jean across from her, so they could still talk. Aunt Rusty stood outside with her warm coat thrown over her shoulders. She was still there, waving, even as the bus turned the corner. I kept looking at her until she disappeared. Then I felt sick, my stomach cramping, my head hurting as the bus pulled out of the familiar driveway.

That day at school and for the next week, I threw up each time I ate the butterscotch pudding with the small, pink candy in the middle. I had the pudding every day because I loved to see the pink candy in the sea of golden butterscotch. I didn't want to take a nap along with the others. Linda, one of the student teachers, was my only friend, but she was busy with so many others. Every once in a while, I began to tell Linda about what happened to my parents, but then decided I didn't want to. The desire to tell her was fleeting; a part of me believed that if I told the truth as I knew it, then it would all go away, like the way my name vanished on the lift-up pad. The bathrobe, the burned grass, all those images that entered my mind, especially when I lay down for a nap without my sister or aunt nearby. But I was older now, and I knew that what had happened was not going to vanish. So I kept my thoughts to myself.

After the first week of school, Aunt Rusty and Uncle Louis were not happy with me. "You need to listen more at school. At nap time everyone is quiet. You don't have to sleep, but just rest and be quiet. Okay?"

When they said this, I looked away, my eyes welling with tears. "I have so many thoughts going on in my mind I can't rest," I blurted out.

"Well, you'll just have to put most of the thoughts away, like in a shut drawer. Just concentrate on what you need to do at the moment. Don't think so much!"

Later that evening, Anne showed me something she had written:

> *My Daddy is a doctor and my Mommy is a nurse. They were burned in a fire and are far away in a hospital. They might not come out of the hospital. I like Sherburne. I live with Robert and Jean, my cousins and my sister, Weezie. We play a lot in the field and now in the snow.*

"Weezie," Annie said, "I wrote this in class today."

"Is Daddy still a doctor?"

"I guess so," she said, her voice flat.

I went over to the green couch where Anne was doing homework and lay next to her, holding my baby doll against my cheek, rubbing it up and down, up and down. I put my head on Anne's shoulder. Anne reached up her hand and lightly touched the top of my head, and I felt very tired.

"It's okay, Weezie," she said, trying to sound like a mother, but she seemed tired too.

On Christmas morning it was snowing. Thick, lacy flakes coated the windowpanes. When Anne and I woke, we didn't spend an extra minute warming ourselves under the double woolen blankets. Instead, we bolted out of bed and raced down the stairs to find presents, many of them sent by nurses at the hospital and friends of our parents'.

Aunt Rusty had made pancakes for everyone. As we sat around the long table, Christmas music playing in the background, all four of us glanced at the tree.

"Can I open one now?" I asked Aunt Rusty, who for once had left the dirty dishes in the sink and moved over toward the tree. She and Uncle Louis were reading the gift cards along with Robert, Jean, and Anne.

"Look at this!" I said after tearing open the wrapping on my first package, a box wrapped in silver paper and decorated with holly. "A pretty shirt!"

"Thanks for the model airplane," Robert said, looking at the intricate pieces. Jean got the doll she had wanted for a long time, the one with long, red braids like hers and a red-and-white pinafore. Anne got skis, which she could hardly wait to put on. We both got warm, woolen dresses, fancy mittens, and pink patent leather purses with black velvet bows. We seemed to be opening more presents than anyone else, one box after another.

"Any more for me?" Jean said.

"That's it, Jean," Aunt Rusty said, looking tired as she surveyed the gifts still left to open.

"What pretty mittens," Anne said, opening up a pair of rose-colored mittens with white deer crocheted onto them.

"And look at my scarf!" I shrieked, unwrapping a long, blue-and-white-striped scarf that wrapped around my neck at least three times and matched my warm, blue jacket.

Anne and I continued unwrapping while everyone else watched.

"Here, Aunt Rusty," I said, handing her a child's cosmetic case with play lipstick, perfume, and nail polish. "I'll play dress up later."

Jean stood up and yawned, gathered her new toys, books, and dolls, and went to her room to play.

Uncle Louis collected the wrapping strewn over the living room floor. General had crawled over near the presents and was now asleep with a red bow tied on his collar and a new bone at his side, a present that Robert had opened for him.

"Anne and Louise," Uncle Louis said, "please take your packages up to your room. We'll sort through everything tomorrow."

Annie and I made at least four trips up the stairs, carrying all our gifts, though Annie's shiny, wooden skis with the red and blue designs on them stayed in the living room. Uncle Louis helped Robert put together the model airplane. Jean came out of her room to play with Anne before bed.

That night, I could feel Della running her fingers

through my hair, singing her sad Irish songs, using pink ribbons, like the ones on the presents, to tie up my ponytail. Later, I could sense my mother rocking me to sleep on her lap, her soft cheek next to mine, singing her made-up song, "Go to sleep, my baby, go to sleep. Go to sleep, my baby, go to sleep." I could see my dad coming through the door in his long, black, woolen coat, putting down his leather doctor bag, and picking me up in his arms and swinging me over his head and then down. I remembered sitting on his lap as he read to me, sometimes the same book again and again so I could learn the words, or at least try to memorize them to sound smart.

The life that Anne and I had lived before was coming back to me: the ballerinas dancing the Nutcracker Suite at City Center, the tiny girls appearing out of the lady's skirt; outings to Schraftts, carrying white muffs and wearing woolen coats with small velvet collars; Christmas parties at Peter Cooper, my mother and father sitting across from each other in armchairs, chatting with friends, as Della carried plates of pigs in a blanket to the guests. The packages from Lord & Taylor, Macy's, and Saks Fifth Avenue had released so many memories. I was torn between two worlds, torn like the expensive wrapping paper, wanting so much to want my parents but feeling like I was leaving them more and more each day.

Chapter Eighteen

On Christmas Day, my father sat in the wooden rocking chair in the middle of the living room of Peter Cooper and stared out the window at the barren trees.

He reached up his damaged right hand and felt his right ear, the one that had been burned half off in the fire. He remembered running up the ladder, his hands burning, the skin slipping off them, attached by threads, as delicate as a spiderweb—one light touch and it fell. As he had rolled in the grass, the pain in his hands had caused him to cover his ears, as if to shut out the noise of the world: my mother's screams, the incessant slapping of the waves across the street. A soundless world would be a painless world. He had touched his right ear and felt a clump of skin fall off into the grass; he had known he was dying piece by piece.

My mother was in the hospital for another in the series of more than thirty operations she would undergo. The staff brought her a turkey dinner with a linen napkin. She could eat small bites of solid food now, as long as she was watched. She heard carolers sing in the morning— "Jingle Bells," "Silent Night," "Hark! The Herald Angels Sing"—though the children, girls in pretty dresses and boys in suits and ties, stayed outside her door so they wouldn't see her badly scarred face.

Nancy, my best friend and neighbor, had seen her many times when her mom, Bunny Moran, had helped my mother with her bandages, with eating, and consoled her when my father was reading one sad book after another and doing little else. At first Nancy ran away when she saw my mother and had trouble sleeping. When Nancy and I were grown-up, she told me that she had clutched her mother at night and always thought she smelled gas during that time. But as the weeks went by, Nancy would slink out to the kitchen searching for ice cream and even sit with our mothers in the living room. She remembered that my mother had once been so pretty, so beautifully dressed, so competent and confident.

January went by slowly. At least Bunny Moran, Helaine Honig, and other neighbors, along with the constant calls from her colleagues at work, helped to bolster my mother's spirits. The phone calls to Anne and me were also going better, but each time she hung up the receiver on Saturday, my mother was desolate. Each call seemed so short, such a small window of time to talk with her children, who seemed to be adjusting to farm life, almost too well, she thought, secretly jealous of Rusty. What she missed most were the ordinary things of life: tucking us into bed, running our bathwater and putting in the bubbles, asking us about school, and buying us clothes to fit our ever-growing bodies.

*

My father's mood continued its downward slide, even though there was the hope of spring and the hope of our return. He still sat in his rocking chair each afternoon. He thought about the seasons. Christmas had come and gone. January had gone, too, the coldest month. Would spring ever come? He thought about the rains of March and the brown sparrows. In early spring, the neighborhood children would cut worms apart in the mud puddles to see if they would regrow, severed twins of life. The sounds of the sparrows would merge with the sounds of the children—their laughing voices bouncing off red brick—but even the voices of his own children could not bring my father back.

He stared at the skin on his hands, which he obsessively peeled, layer by layer, so little white shreds, like bits of coconut, fell on the beige carpet. He hoped the carpet would camouflage the detritus, but sometimes, afraid that at some point in the future his children would walk barefoot across the rug and get pieces of his skin stuck to the soles of their young feet, he reached down and pulled up pieces of himself from the wooly carpet. Perhaps he was trying to get back to the skin before the accident; perhaps if he went down far enough, picking at himself like a vulture picks at carrion, he could recover his soft, smooth skin.

At such moments he thought of his wife, but always as she was before the fire. He knew that when he looked at her now, he couldn't help what his eyes expressed. He was revolted by her scarred face. He also felt horribly guilty that he was not burned as badly; that she had suffered the brunt of it.

Though he was not one of those men who constantly primped in front of the mirror, he knew, as a Jew in a Christian world, and having been a token Jewish student at Yale with all the well-dressed WASPs and their well-dressed families, how much appearance mattered. He liked his Brooks Bothers suits. He was particular about his hair, how it was cut: short on the sides, longer in the back. He went to the same barber every three weeks on 53rd Street, right near Health Insurance Plan. He was "doc" to Gene, his Italian barber. When the haircut was finished, Gene handed my father a big, round mirror and turned the chair around so he could look at himself, first from the front, and then from the back, remarking how every hair was in place. "A good cut," my father always said, tipping him just a little bit extra, nothing extravagant. At home, his new electric razor gave him a reasonably good (if sometimes less than perfect) shave. "I don't want you looking like one of the alcoholic men at the Salvation Army," my mother would say to my father, secretly thrilled to have a husband who took as good care of himself as she took of herself. That was something they shared—good looks and attention to detail.

So when my mother, her face almost unrecognizable, her arm attached to her face with a pedicle of flesh, entered the room each day she was at home, his whole body shifted as if under the weight of some collapse. At night when he went to sleep, he glanced at her in the twin bed beside his and felt a numbness overtake him.

That morning, my mother was home between operations and a nurse took her to physical therapy. He sat in his rocking chair and tried to read, but it seemed that not only the words but also his eyes ran together. He knew now was the time, if it was ever to happen. He got up carefully, more determined than he had been in months, and walked into the bathroom. He could feel himself walking, as if he had already begun not to belong to himself; he would soon belong to the air. This float-ing feeling was new, and he hoped it was a precursor to what would come if he were ever granted an afterlife. The beige carpet felt soft underneath his feet, and for the first time he really looked around the living room. He saw the dark-brown bookshelves, displaying the books that meant so much to him: *Einstein: The Life and Times*, *A Picasso Retrospective*, a three-volume set of Freud, and the *Alice in Wonderland* he gave to my mother on Christmas, 1946. For her "entertainment and lasting friendship with Alice," he had written in the book on their first Christmas together after he came home from the war. That evening, she read him the beginning of the first chapter, when Alice goes down the rabbit hole into a never-ending adventure, "never once considering how in the world she was to get out again."

He still had a sensation of floating, of turning into air, all his molecules soaring to some unknown height. For a moment he felt he might become a bird. He would bring messages down to his family and watch over them. Suddenly he felt like crying but held it in. He turned right into the bathroom and opened the medicine cabinet. My mother had all her sleeping pills on the second shelf, just as he remembered. He opened the bottle and counted them one by one. As a doctor, he knew how many to take, but he started trembling, suddenly unsure of the dosage. He closed the door to the cabinet and glimpsed his face in the mirror. He knew how badly my mother had been burned, but when he looked at his face—the vacant eyes, the half ear, the half eyebrows—he saw how damaged he, too, had been by the explosion.

Perhaps he had brought all this on himself. Had he been kind enough to his own parents? For weeks, he had plunged into the book of Job and dwelled endlessly on his past. His father had died of cancer when my father had been a captain in the army in Persia. He hadn't even asked for leave to be with his mother and comfort her. When the Red Cross had said she was fine, he had believed them and gone about his duties. How could she have been fine with one son already dead, her husband now gone as well, and her remaining son at war? How awful, tragic, really, that he hadn't asked for a leave. Of course they would have given it to him. He was a captain, for God's sake! Why didn't he just ask?

His poor mother with her broken English. While the other guys at Yale invited their parents up for the weekend, or to the yearly party in New York, he threw the gold-embossed invitations into the trash. A lot of the guys, mostly WASPs, had wealthy, educated parents who dressed in tailored gowns and suits and spoke impeccable English. What would they think of Herm? What would they whisper to each other when shy, insecure Lena— obese, dressed in a brightly colored tent dress, look- ing like a Russian immigrant—walked into the room? Why hadn't he embraced her in all her fleshy warmth, introduced her to his friends, and told them that his mom and dad's hard work and love had made it possible for him to go to Yale? To succeed? What was that?

He remembered his brother, Philip, sweet, fun Philip—the two of them jumping waves at Jones Beach, talking late into the night about girls. Philip came home from Brown University. He was "not well." By the time he was treated, his fate had been sealed: kidney failure. "Make him comfortable," the doctors said. Case closed. My father gave Philip blood, and then counseled him that it was silly to marry his Paterson High School sweetheart. "Not a good idea," my father said to his younger brother, knowing he would probably die. Why had my father convinced his brother not to marry? Why didn't he stand as his best man, even if in a room on the 20th floor of Mt. Sinai Hospital, letting his brother go knowing he was loved, and letting Rachel, his girlfriend, give herself. She was young and pretty. She would probably marry again. How stupid, stupid, stupid, my father thought to himself.

Maybe he had been a bad person. Maybe he was being punished. Now there were no more chances to make it up to them. His mother had died of complications from diabetes in a Lower East Side tenement, a two-story walk-up. He had been saving to move her to a nicer place—perhaps even to Peter Cooper. She would have had grandchildren to take to the playgrounds and push on the swings. They hadn't even told her that Dorothy was pregnant. They had decided to wait until the fourth month, when there are fewer risks of miscarriage. Dorothy was older and had had trouble getting pregnant. It was right to wait, wasn't it? But Lena Zevin died before she could learn the good news. He got the call in the afternoon at his East 86th Street office and drove as fast as he could to the Lower East Side. She was lying in bed, her open eyes, startled and sad at the same time. An old Jewish prayer book, pictures of her husband, and her two boys, Philip and Herman, were next to her bed. She had on a flowered muumuu. Her flesh—the enormous amount of flesh that enveloped her—was now cold. He listened to her chest, closed her eyes, and pronounced his own mother dead. Waves of guilt swept over him, guilt for his first family and now for the accident.

Holding the pills in his hand, he sat on his bed, near the telephone. He would finally join his brother and their parents. But what would his brother think? His brother had had no choice, and if he had been offered the choice, he would have chosen life. My father put the pills down on the bed. He looked at how small and round they were and knew how bitter they would taste. The bitterness would be momentary; death would be forever. He shivered. Waves of nausea overcame him, and he felt dizzy. He remembered he had one important phone call to make. Going to his file cabinet in the bedroom closet, he pulled out the file marked Life Insurance. His hands shook as he read through the policy one more time. He could find nothing about suicide, even though he knew the answer. Why would an insurance company pay for a suicide? His eyes teared up. How would Dorothy cope? How would his children cope? As he read the pages, his eyes were drawn to a black-and-white snapshot of himself with Anne. Her eyes were creased with joy, her bathing suit wet from racing in the waves. He was holding her hand tightly. He tried to remember that grip. And where was his Weezie? So little still, so much a baby. He turned his face away and dialed the number.

"Hello. State Farm," a voice said from the other line.

"Hello," my father said, suddenly feeling awkward and embarrassed. "My name is Dr. Nayer, and I have a patient who is severely depressed and keeps wanting to know if State Farm will pay money to the family if he commits suicide. I'm not sure what to say to my patient."

"Hold on a minute, will you, Dr. Nayer?" There was a long pause and he could hear voices in the background. He glanced at the clock and began to fear that my mother would soon return.

"No. Life insurance companies, at least ours, never pay for suicide," the woman said. "I hope he gets better," she added softly.

"Thank you." His body suddenly stiffened as if a knife had cut him in two. Like a worm struggling for life in its half-existence, he made his way back to his rocking chair with the pills in his pocket, stopping only to get the Bible down from the bookshelf, and started reading the book of Job. This time, he turned to the ending. "Job lived one hundred and forty years and saw his sons and his son's sons and even four generations. So Job died being old and full of days." All the darkness could be lifted, he thought. It was possible. He hadn't done it. He held his hands tightly together, the right in the left, and squeezed himself back to life.

*

At Beth Israel Hospital, my mother was in for yet another operation to move the pedicle and slowly spread the skin across her face. But when she was admitted, there was a delay. The skin had a slightly bluish tone. It might not be viable anymore. My mother, always adept at holding in her tears, felt like she was going to explode in grief and anger. This setback would mean additional weeks, maybe months, before she could pick up her children. Dr. Barsky told her how much time it would take, but she hardly heard his words as she stared at the calendar on the wall.

"You'll need to stay overnight while we check on you," he said, and she fell back into her pillow with all the weight of her small body.

The second-floor room at Beth Israel, with its green-speckled linoleum floor and beige walls, was warm, but my mother was cold. She was suddenly sick and tired of it all, sick and tired of her husband. What if Hank didn't go back to work? How would they live? Would he ever stop complaining and whining for long enough to think of that? Did he think of the children? How could he be so selfish?

As her anger rose, it pushed her into action. She and my father had done everything exactly as Stella Chess had suggested, calling the children on Saturday evenings, always at the same time. The calls had improved. Anne talked about school, about her singing performance, about what she did each day. She had sung "Billy Boy" in front of all of Sherburne School, "Where have you been,

Billy Boy, Billy Boy, O where have you been, charming Billy?" and ending with "She's a young girl and cannot leave her mother." Weezie got on the phone, too, now talking with both her mom and dad.

But why couldn't she call them "out of turn?" Why couldn't she call her children whenever she wanted to? She wanted more contact and resented the once-a-week restriction. They were her children, after all. She had given birth to them and she should be able to call them when she wanted. She had been so good and listened to everything Stella Chess had to say. She didn't have to do what professionals told her anymore. She hadn't lived her life just to be told what to do. Fueled by a new and deep disappointment, one that would mean delaying yet again their reunion with the children, she decided that playing by the rules—rules dictated by others who were not in hospital beds separated from their children for months—was simply not working. She'd had enough. She would call when she felt like it. Her mind was rattling now as she picked up the receiver and dialed.

It was a Tuesday night at the end of February when the phone rang. Aunt Rusty walked over to the phone table and picked up the receiver and looked surprised. We were all sitting in the living room. She talked softly for a few minutes, then handed the phone to Anne, who grabbed the receiver with the look of a wild animal. It wasn't Saturday. Why would they be calling? I listened to every word my sister said.

"Hi, Mommy, I have to write a paragraph on my favorite thing to do. I'm not sure what to write about . . . Okay.

I could write about ice-skating in Central Park . . . "

"Where's Daddy? Where is he?" Anne asked, her voice sounding more frantic. I sat on the edge of the couch, nervously twisting a piece of Kleenex between my fingers. My aunt and uncle were looking at each other.

"But he is always in the hospital room with you. Where is he, Mommy?" I didn't know what my mother said then, but Anne starting screaming into the phone.

"My daddy's dead," Anne said, handing the phone to Uncle Louis. "My daddy's dead," she said louder now, sobbing. "I don't have a daddy anymore."

I jumped up from the living room couch where I had been writing a list of words and stood near my sister, watching her every move for clues about the truth. Everything was becoming clear: our mother's and father's voices sounded different; the handwriting curved too far to the right; the presents were sent by nurses, not by our parents; no pictures of our mother and father were shown because it wouldn't be right to display pictures of the dead; conversations had become hushed when we entered the room, beginning with the week we stayed at the Simons'. Quietness, whispers, muted sounds, secrets. No one had ever told us the truth. No one had a picture of our mom and dad on their bureau. No one. Even our grandparents talked little about what had happened. They all knew something that they weren't telling us, and it was obvious, oh so obvious to Anne. We had seen the truth: the burned bathrobe without Daddy inside it, which appeared in my dreams. He had been vaporized, leaving behind a covering, a piece of cloth that now had no father smell but only a burned smell. And the grass was burned, too. They had to be dead. Anne knew it, and I knew it, too.

"Weezie. Your mother's on the phone," Aunt Rusty said. But I was now lying near Anne, who was sobbing.

"It's not really her," I said, feeling guilty that I wasn't coming to the phone. "I'm not talking. I'm with Annie."

Anne, who was lying down on the couch with me holding onto her, suddenly lifted herself up and sat up as straight as she could and tried to breathe, but only a deep, wheezing sound filled the room. The congestion in her lungs made it hard for her to breathe, as if she was breathing in through a straw with an opening so small that nothing would reach her lungs. I ran in circles around the room, like a moth circling a bulb, not knowing what to do.

"Robert," Uncle Louis shouted, "go upstairs and find the medicine marked Anne Nayer! Now!"

Then Uncle Louis called the doctor, who lived ten miles away, while Aunt Rusty massaged Anne's chest. "Calm down, Anne," Aunt Rusty said. It had always worked before; whenever Anne began to wheeze, Aunt Rusty would say, "Stop," and Anne would stop. But this time the wheezing was too deep; her chest was plugged with mucus.

"Will Anne be okay?" Jean asked, bringing her cousin water.

"She'll be fine," Aunt Rusty said, though her eyes looked scared.

I sat near her, praying. *God bless Annie and make her better soon. God Bless Annie and make her better soon.* I was terrified I would lose her, too.

"My daddy's dead," Anne whispered, the only words she got out as she tried to suck in air. "My daddy's dead," she whispered again. "Dead. Dead. Dead."

"Your daddy's not dead. He'll come get you soon. Soon." Aunt Rusty said.

Robert rushed down with the medicine. Aunt Rusty stopped massaging Anne's chest and gave her a teaspoon of the medicine. For a few minutes, there was an eerie quiet in the room, punctuated only by the sound of Anne's rasping. Even General had turned his head away from the kitchen, switching positions so he could look at Anne with his round, brown eyes. Everyone was staring at her and silently praying. Sherburne was a small town, far from a doctor, and at least forty minutes from the nearest hospital.

By now Anne was using her stomach muscles to breathe. Her skin was pasty and her lips were beginning to turn blue, like she had been in the cold water too long.

"Your lips are blue. Come back," Daddy would say to Anne at the beach on Cape Cod. She would run into Daddy's arms like she ran into the water, with wild abandon, and stay there.

"Your lips are blue. Come back," I said to my sister. "Come back."

A few minutes later, everyone breathed a sigh of relief. Anne's cheeks began to flood with a light-pink hue. The doctor arrived some time later.

"She's tired," Dr. Stevens said, "very tired. She must have had quite a bad attack. Let her rest for tonight, and no school tomorrow. If she continues wheezing, give her a teaspoon of the medicine every four to six hours. Call me if she still has trouble breathing."

That night, I kept looking at Annie to make sure she was breathing. I heard my uncle call my mother and tell her Anne had had a bad asthma attack, that she thought her daddy was dead.

Alarmed and confused after that phone call, my parents called Stella Chess again.

"Anything that upsets the tenuous belief that you and Hank still love them and are alive must be avoided," she had said. "Anything out of the ordinary could send the children spinning into a tumultuous world."

My mother now knew she had to act. The children would have to come back as soon as she could figure it all out. Her daughters could no longer be protected from her scarred face and hands. She had trouble grasping doorknobs, cooking, opening jars and bottles. So what? She would ask for help. Her children could help her. They were her children, and they belonged with her, now. Her hands would get better; she would make sure of it. She could even write a little now. She had been writing three words a day with her right hand. She would write perfectly in a year. She could hold Anne's and Weezie's hands when they crossed the street. That much she could do. It didn't matter what she looked like. This phoning "out of turn" would only lead her children back to her. Maybe Della would come back. She was with another family now, but Della had said that she would always come back. Maybe she could work it out. She would have to work it out!

But one thing was missing: my father. My father had been slowly detaching himself from the world for months. He was always preoccupied, still in his rocking chair looking out the window, reading one morbid story after another, and still asking *why*. What a silly, useless question, she thought. The past can't be changed, so why go back there? It's the present that is important.

What if he refused to get on the train to get his children? She knew what had to be done. Even if my father had lost his will to live, the children had to come home. He had no choice. He would go to Sherburne. She reached over to her night table, opened the drawer, pulled out a lined pad and a thick pencil, and struggled to write. It took her over an hour, but she was amazed that she could make a list: 1. Find Della. 2. Call P.S. 40 and enroll children. 3. Get Anne and Louise's room in order. 4. Ask Peggy or Bunny to get them clothes. Check with Rusty on sizes. As my mother made her list, she felt her spirits rise.

The next morning, Peggy Rennison came to take my mother home. My mother's arm was raised up in a sling again, another attempt at a pedicle that would be spread across her face. She prayed that this time it would work. Peggy had brought my mother a red woolen button-down dress with a neck that could be pulled up for warmth and also cover her scars. For extra coverage, she brought a green-and-red silk scarf.

"Did you see Hank yesterday?" my mother asked.

"Yes. Not much change."

My mother told Peggy about the phone call. "We

can't wait any longer. I'm not asking Hank to pick up the girls, I'm telling him: he has to pick up his children or move out. I've had enough of his moods!"

The air was beginning to get warmer. The new colors of March began to show themselves, like a peacock spreading its wings. The ancient, gray rocks appeared on the hills, released from the weight of the constant snow that had camouflaged them. The cows were spending more time out of the barn, milling on the grass, their black-and-white coats glistening in the sun.

In the autumn we had buried mica by the rocks. Soon we would be able to search for our treasure—the sparkling glass and fragile mirrors of mica—and see if it had survived under the weight of one of the coldest winters in upstate New York.

"Let's take this home and scare Mom!" Robert hollered one weekend afternoon when we were playing by the rocks. He carefully held a garter snake, its head in his hands, carrying it behind his back on the walk through the field to the house. Aunt Rusty was washing dishes, lost in thought.

Robert walked in first, his tall body towering over his mom's. We crept silently behind him; Jean, Anne, and I clustered together like three pirates. Robert walked up to Aunt Rusty and bent over to give her a kiss, dangling the snake behind her back. Suddenly, he thrust the snake in front of her face, and she let out a high-pitched scream as we all fell on the linoleum floor, laughing.

"Don't ever do that again! Do you hear?" she yelled at him, her face red, her hands cupped together as soap smeared her red apron. "I could have had a heart attack!"

Robert put his right hand on his mother's shoulder. "I'm sorry, Ma."

We ran out the door and lay on the gray rocks until lunchtime.

At noon, Anne and I were seated at the small, wooden kitchen table eating peanut butter and jelly sandwiches. Jean and Robert were out with their dad. Aunt Rusty, standing near the sink, folded the newspaper she was reading; we heard the crinkling of the paper and saw the sunlight coming in from the window, lighting up her rust-colored hair.

"Your father is coming to get you in a week," she said to us, directly facing Anne and me. "We'll need to get everything packed and sent back to New York City. Your mother and father will be out of the hospital."

I felt my stomach drop to the floor as if an iron ball had hit me in the middle: I was a building being gutted. I looked down at my fingers and noticed they had grown bigger and stronger. Beyond them, the gold sparkles on the linoleum floor started to swirl, and I almost moved, as if in a trance, to the place where I used to vomit each morning, to the place where I stopped throwing up because now I was part of these walls, this life with my aunt and uncle and cousins.

Anne shifted excitedly in her seat, her eyes moving in all directions. I swung my foot back and forth under the table.

"Stop kicking me, Weezie," she said, annoyed, and I began to cry. Then I controlled my tears and sat silently.

"Now remember, when you see your mother, don't say anything about how she looks."

We were silent.

"When is Daddy coming?" Anne said. "Should we pack? Will Mommy be home when we get there?" Anne rattled off question after question until Aunt Rusty told us to play outside while she finished her chores.

When we went outside, Anne ran far ahead, and I could see her climbing the rocks without me. "Stop, Annie, stop!" I yelled. But Anne didn't want to look back, and I suddenly wanted no one, not my sister, not my mother, not my father. All I wanted was Shep and the crickets and my aunt and the run of the fields.

Chapter Nineteen

In early March of 1955, my father got off the train in Utica, New York, where Uncle Louis was waiting for him.

When my mother had given him the ultimatum only a couple of weeks before, he had packed a small bag with great effort, made some calls, and mustered up the only hope left in him—his children.

That morning before he left, he reached up his hand to the part of his ear that was missing, like a socket where a tooth once lived. Then he felt his thin, tightly stretched facial skin, like an egg-white mask. He looked at his face for a longer time than usual, trying to see it as his children would, searching through the brown spots, the shiny grafts, the white patches where no blood seemed to flow. How dead he would look to them.

"Just do it," my mother kept saying from a mouth full of scars. "Stop thinking so much about how you look, or what they will think. Just do it! Get them. Bring them home."

He knew what she knew but couldn't say except in the middle of the night when they both tossed and turned, sometimes crying out in their sleep, the loss so palpable, so complete. In the morning they woke to photos of the girls on their bureau. The photos were static; no one grew or changed. At that point he knew his wife was right: if another week, another day, or too many more hours went by, their daughters might be permanently lost to them. Their daughters' hearts would become the hearts of orphans, each one a candy that would swirl around and around one hard layer after the next, the soft middle just a pinprick.

When Uncle Louis opened the door to the white farmhouse, there were two forces at work. One was the chill wind that rushed in from outside, and the other was my father, returning for his two daughters after nearly nine horrifying months. He was changed in the way that people are changed when they come back from war, or lose a child, or lose their minds; he was changed well beyond the mottled, shiny skin of yellow, brown, and ivory or the half-burned-off eyebrows that would have expressed constant surprise if it hadn't been for the sorrow that sucked away his soul.

After the door was closed behind him, my father—his shoulders stooped, his head down, his black-gloved hands still in his pocket—stared at Anne and me, his daughters, who appeared so cozy and settled in this new family. He took a deep breath and a few tentative steps toward his girls. For a minute the room was unbelievably silent, even though seven people inhabited the small space.

Aunt Rusty, sensing the profound awkwardness, took his coat. "I'll go make hot chocolate for the children and some coffee for you. You must be tired after such a long trip." He nodded.

"Anne, Louise," he said, his voice thin like it had been on the telephone for all those months. "Anne, Louise—how you've grown!"

That Anne and I did not immediately rise from the floor when the door opened and that our father, our daddy, did not swoop us up in his arms created a heaviness in the room, a paralyzing blanket of thick air. Anne, who had just acquired Park Place in the game of Monopoly before the knock at the door, seemed to lift her whole body off the ground without actually moving, a kind of stiff attempt at flight. I had been dreaming and praying for this day to arrive, reciting nightly "God bless Mommy and Daddy," and now here he was, in the flesh, standing in the doorway. I took in the simple warmth of the farm-house and looked over at my beloved General, whose familiar brown-and-white body was sprawled across the heater. That day I had finally washed the dishes myself; Jean and Anne had praised me. I had been growing up without my father and mother; suddenly, my father was here. I held my hands together now, as if I wanted to pray or make a fist. The room remained eerily quiet, everyone waiting for something big that would change all the sorrow of that Saturday night into joy. Daddy was back. This was the moment we had been waiting for.

Awkwardly standing in his woolen coat, Daddy moved toward us. My mind was racing back and forth—from my father, so oddly sad, to the marshmallows that would soon be floating in a sea of chocolate, and back again to my father, almost a stranger now with his heavy-lidded eyes.

Finally, Anne and I rose from the floor and held hands.

"Weezie, Annie," he said again, his voice rising up out of a drowning place, trying so hard to rise to the surface. "Weezie, Annie, how you've grown!"

"Hi, Daddy," Anne said, moving toward him first. "Where's Mommy?"

"You'll see her tomorrow," he said, his voice breaking. "She's at home."

At the word "home," Anne and I went to the green couch and our father followed us. Jean and Robert had gone into the kitchen. General picked himself up and shuffled over to me, sitting right under my feet, which now almost touched the floor when I sat on the couch.

"I brought a book to read," he said, pulling a book out of his suitcase.

"Where's your doctor bag?" I asked, wanting to smell the familiar antiseptic scent of the black leather bag that he always carried home with him.

"The bag's in the closet at home. I haven't used it in a long time."

He looked down at the book. Then he began to read, the old voice hidden but still discernible behind a black shroud. At each word we moved closer and closer to him on the couch. I could see the effort in his hands because they were trembling slightly. I tried not to look at them: white, knobby flesh protruded from parts of his thin, yellowy skin. At times he stopped mid-sentence and looked first at Anne and then at me, as if drinking in our faces. Anne seemed to be trying to find him, to pull him back to her, like searching for the mica that we had hidden under the snow, something fragile that the four of us hoped had survived the long winter.

The morning was a rush of suitcases. Just like when we arrived, Robert and Uncle Louis carried our suitcases to the car. My uncle hugged me for a long time and I smelled his flannel shirt. My aunt cried and held Anne and me as my father said, "It's time to go." My father was quiet, almost silent, on the way to the train station. We boarded the train and gazed out its thick, dusty windows. As we rode through the town of Sherburne, I watched my school, the one-room schoolhouse with the slide in the middle, disappear into the distance.

When we sat down together in the daylight, I could see my daddy better. His face and his hands were shiny and deathlike, something like his eyes. His eyes were always on the verge of tears, even as he ordered a roast beef sandwich and a Coke for Anne, and a chicken sandwich and a ginger ale for me. I stared out the window aimlessly, remembering the smell of the Yorkshire pudding my uncle made for Sunday dinner.

"You can say anything you want to about your mother's face," he said, for the first time looking directly at Anne and me. We were silent.

The sound of the elevator rising from the first floor usually went unnoticed, but today it was the sound my mother hung on to with every breath. On this day she listened for the sound of her whole life being returned to her. The train had arrived on schedule at 2:00 p.m. She had called to find out. The cab ride would take twenty minutes, or perhaps a little more with the wait at Grand

Central. She envisioned my father holding the suitcases and Annie and I standing next to him. My mother did not let herself drift into thoughts of what we would think, as my father had done day after day. She was our mother. We would have to adjust, just as she had adjusted.

When the train pulled into Grand Central Station, the cacophony of sounds was almost unbearable to Anne and me. We had lived for more than eight months among snowdrifts and vast fields. Here, vendors shouted out, "Get the *Daily News*, hot off the press!" Shoeshine men yelled, "Get a shine, get a shine!" People rushed by, moving in a million directions, and Daddy yelled along with everyone else—"Hang on to me!"—as we waded through the scores of people in the crowded terminal. He held my hand too tightly, squeezing my fingers together, but I didn't say anything. I glanced at Anne. She was leaning toward Daddy, but I sensed she felt, as I did, that his hands weren't soft anymore but as thin as parchment, yellowed, and slightly bent. As we walked through the crowds, I looked up at the ceiling. A flying horse with yellow wings and stars in his hooves covered the domed ceiling. His eye was dusted with yellow like a spring flower.

"Why is that horse flying?" I asked, as my father kept moving. He stopped for a moment and looked up at the ceiling.

"That's Pegasus," he said, "a mythical horse that flies. You can see him in the sky. I'll show you sometime." My father's voice was flatter than I had ever remembered it, but I was excited that someday I would see Pegasus in the sky.

"This way to the street," he said, trying to pull us out of the chaos of the station.

We were mesmerized, stunned by the squawking noises that just eight months before had been a part of our landscape. The street was more of a shock than the station. Concrete stretched endlessly, without grass or flowers to grace the eternal gray. Buildings shot up into the sky. The fields of Sherburne were gone; Shep was gone; General was gone; Aunt Rusty, Uncle Louis, and Jean and Robert were gone.

When the taxi drove into Peter Cooper Village, Daddy waved at the security guard. "Hi, doc," the guard said, smiling broadly. "I see you've got your girls."

The driver stopped in front of 4 Peter Cooper Road. The red brick of the buildings brought us back to the place before the accident. Annie and I walked ahead of Daddy to the bright elevator. I just wanted my mommy, the scent of her, her steady voice, her dark jewel eyes and milky English complexion with a hint of rouge on her cheeks. I wanted to touch her wavy, light-brown hair, her small, thin hands, and slightly round stomach, which I remembered sitting against as we watched the waves break in Wellfleet, mother and daughter, mouths filled with pink lemonade and the taste of sea salt.

"I can almost reach the doorbell," I said gleefully to my father as he took off his right glove, exposing the burned skin, opened his black leather key chain and turned the key in the lock.

Anne, standing close to him, had tightened all her facial muscles. As the door opened, we both saw a woman whose left arm was raised painfully in the air, and when

I got closer I could see a doughy mass, a fleshy tunnel of skin that was attached from her left arm to her face. The left sleeve of her blue Chinese jacket hung limp. Her face was ravaged by ropy scars and ugly rivulets below her eyes. Her right eye was bigger than the left, and no real eyebrows arched protectively above them, only thin pencil lines. Her right hand, twisted and deformed, looked like it was permanently grasping for something. All I could think when I first saw her was that if I had known, I would have run back to the farm and to my aunt, to a mother who wasn't burned. If it hadn't been for the familiar living room, the old smells, and my mother's voice—still and steady, trying so hard—I still might have run.

"You look terrible, Mommy," I said, standing near her.

"Mommy doesn't look so bad," Anne lied, also moving near her.

Her right hand, which I wanted to hold, was a claw. Now my mother rested her face in her right hand so most of it was covered as she continued to stare at us.

Exactly what happened in those moments is a blur, but Anne and I both realized that giving and getting love would no longer be easy. We couldn't run up and kiss our mother's face because it looked so ugly that it made us want to run away. We couldn't take her hands because they were scarred and crippled. And she couldn't go to Anne and me and hug us because she saw her own ugliness reflected in our eyes.

Chapter Twenty

When Dr. Rhodes told me I needed more sessions than Kaiser could provide, I went about looking for a new therapist; I found Nina Lathrop, a psychoanalyst trained in Freudian theory who would work miracles on my life. She knew Anna Freud and had visited her in Europe. I put a lot of faith in her. At the very moment I first saw her, I wanted to rid my body of the screaming panic that threatened to disable me, to keep me from crossing bridges, from driving, from calming my shattered nerves.

I'll always remember the smell of her Upper Haight-Ashbury Maybeck house, its musty hominess. Walking into her house was like walking into the woods, with all the dark wood of the floors, walls, and ceilings, and the long, almost medieval table.

Whenever Nina—small, thin, and always sophisticated in a fitted dress, pumps, and jewelry—opened the door, she would look at me lovingly and reach out to take both of my hands in hers. "Please come in," she would say, or, "Please wait in the room. I'll be out in a few minutes." Though I was still revved up from the panic in the first months I saw her, she brought me into another way of being, into her dark-wood, womb-like home with its picture windows overlooking the tree branches, and her African violets, which she diligently tended to even now that she was in her seventies.

As I walked down the hallway to her home office for the first time, I noticed all the books, reminding me of the books I had grown up with in my childhood home: old novels in hardback editions, medical texts, volumes of Freud. That first day, she sat in a large, black chair and told me I could either sit or lie down on the couch. I had never been to a bona fide psychoanalyst before. I decided to sit up, at least for a time, so I could see Nina and look out her windows at the trees.

"I have a patient who burned her house down, her panic attacks were so bad. You're not going to burn your house down, are you?"

I looked at her, a bit shocked, and then smiled. "No, I'm not planning on burning my house down."

"Well, that's good," she said.

Then we began a healing process that would continue for four years and would have gone even longer if Nina hadn't gotten sick. My husband and I had little money then and she saw me "for a song."

"I don't really need the money," she said, "and I want to help you."

I dreamt of everything, including the red brick of Peter Cooper. I had constant dreams of fire, and a recurring dream of water—of the huge, monstrous waves of the Pacific at Land's End. In the dream, I was inside those waves; at first I was always terrified, but by the end of the dream I loved the water and came bobbing up like a fish. I also dreamed of the cellar on Cape Cod; I kept going farther down the ladder. Some days, I felt like killing myself, dreaming of knives cutting me, blood spurting out.

"The knives were always there," Nina said. "Your mother went under the knife many times. You must have felt those knives were cutting into you."

For four years on Monday afternoons I saw Nina. Sometimes when I didn't have a babysitter, I brought my children with me, and she would cup their faces in her hands. "You're so beautiful," she would say. "And you, you are so beautiful, too." They would draw pictures in her waiting room.

I continued to tell her the story of the accident as I was writing it down. I interviewed my mother and father and sister, to help me piece together what had happened as we had reconstructed our lives, as the doctors had reconstructed my mother's face, as my father had found the strength to go on, as we all had entered the world again, forever changed.

My mother's scarred face and hands, her one-sleeved clothes, her new antiseptic smells; my father's slow, underwater voice, his eyes brimming with tears—all that pain was unspoken, silent. So was all the pain of missing my aunt, uncle, and cousins, the hidden mica and the new spring flowers. All the pain was sealed in an envelope, buried in a deep hole, a vault in the walls of our hearts, never to be opened, never to spill out, because it would mar the scheduled plan, the scheduled recovery;

the pain would remind my parents of the chaos that my mother, in particular, was trying so hard to forget. The clothes would be folded, the wrinkles ironed out.

Three times a week at 9:30 a.m., my mother walked out of Peter Cooper Village and set out for physical therapy along the stone-covered serpentine road. She walked on the side of the road where the red-brick buildings cast their shadows, hoping they would make her scars less noticeable. As she passed by the women who sat on the green benches, they cranked their heads in syncopated rhythm and stared. She looked down and gazed at the dried grass, arranged in planters around the buildings, like moats around castles, protected by a border of gray chains. Pretty, not to be trampled on. She liked the order. No one would mar the surface.

My mother passed the security checkpoint and didn't turn left, as she used to. For years, she would first go to the mailbox to mail bills or to mail the letters she wrote every week to her brother and mother in upstate New York and to Eileen, an English friend she had met on a biking trip in Germany in 1933, when she was twenty-five. She and Eileen had been pretty, young women then and had thrown pennies into a fountain in Brugge, hoping for handsome husbands.

She didn't walk left toward Stuyvesant Town and all the stores, the bakery where she and Della had regularly picked up chocolate éclairs with thick custard fillings and a napoleon for my father. She didn't walk to the children's shoe store with the elephant and tiger seats, where Annie and I would sit up high like princesses while the shoe salesman measured our feet. Instead, she faced north toward the United Nations and the gray-brick buildings of First Avenue. Cabs whizzed along the wide, seven-lane boulevard. The occasional bicyclist risked his life among the traffic. Periodically, she heard the sounds of a siren and shuddered. Sometimes my mother would look up from the rocks and cracks in the concrete to watch the people rushing out of the crowded buses that stopped on 23rd Street. As soon as someone saw her face and gasped, she would look down again, hearing the roar of the engine as the bus took its passengers to the next stop. No one realized that she had seen them and was taking in everything: young girls in paisley skirts and button-down oxford shirts, women in handsome, belted shirtwaists and blazers, mothers with small children carefully stepping down from buses. When a child saw her face, he or she would point or cry out. Adults would take a quick look and hold their breaths; she could see their bodies freeze until they turned away and whispered to their companions.

When no one walked by her, she would listen for a moment to the birds, the sparrows that reminded her of spring. Lulled by the birdsong, she would forget for a few seconds that her face had been damaged, until another stranger passed.

At the entrance to the hospital on First Avenue, the stares stopped. She was a regular, this burned lady with her halting walk.

"Hello, Mrs. Nayer," Patty the physical therapist said. "Are you ready for the warm water?"

As my mother put her hands in the water, Patty massaged her fingers and applied heat, trying to loosen up the underlying tissue. She would pull my mother's fingers in the right direction, sometimes using rubber bands to stretch the tendons. Every once in a while, my mother would put her hands in warm wax; she liked the velvety feel of the wax, and with her hands submerged, she couldn't see the damage. Patty would then ask her to open and close her fists, to spread her fingers as wide as she could. Sometimes it hurt and she wanted to cry out, but she had to work through the pain. After a half hour of kneading dough and working with clay, my mother would rinse her hands and have a warm muffin and orange juice, sustenance for the long walk home and the stares.

All of it was exhausting, but she knew she had to move out into the world. They would all get their lives back together, whatever it took. Her children were back. And her husband was slowly coming back to them.

I entered kindergarten in late March, three days after my return from the farm. Belinda, our new babysitter, Anne, Nancy, my best friend, and I walked across First Avenue to P.S. 40. Anne and I were wearing new outfits: brown corduroy skirts, white button-down blouses, and warm, red jackets that insulated us from the cold.

"Don't leave me alone," I cried out to Nancy and Anne when they dropped me off in front of Room 202.

"You'll be fine," Anne whispered in my ear before she and Nancy vanished to their own classrooms.

"It's good to see you, Louise," Mrs. Derrin said as she showed me to the brown circle rug where thirty children gathered. I glanced at the yellow walls, on which each letter of the alphabet was drawn on squares of white paper, a snake curling around the letter S and a lion peeking out of the corner of the letter L.

"First of all, let's welcome Louise, who will be with us for the rest of the year," announced Mrs. Derrin. All eyes stared at me and my teeth clamped down tightly in my jaw. I wanted to disappear into the crack in the wall by the letter Z. I looked down at the brown rug and ran my fingers over the soft wool while the teacher began show-and-tell. A small boy with blond hair jumped up and pulled a brown rock out of the pocket of his blue-jeans.

"My father took a trip to Death Valley and brought this back for me. It came all the way from a desert, way far in the West." He fingered the rock quietly, like a secret, and held it up so all of us could see the dark-brown surface streaked with white.

"Death Valley is here," Mrs. Derrin said, pointing to the map.

Three or four more children got up, stood next to the teacher, and talked. One girl said her Aunt Lucy took her to Boston for the weekend, where she tried lobster and dipped the tail in butter sauce. It gave her a stomachache. I was quite shy but felt compelled to tell my story for the first time, perhaps because I knew it was a bigger and better story than any story that had been told so far. I slowly rose from the floor, walked to where the teacher was standing, and turned around. When I saw the thirty faces staring up at me, I tried to take a deep breath but couldn't. I averted my eyes from my audience and focused on the door, slightly ajar, which led to the hallway where my sister and Nancy had just left me.

"My mommy and daddy were burned in a fire. My mommy's face has lots of scars all over it."

Then I sat down and took my place in the circle. A peculiar silence filled the room. All the children seemed eager to know more. They wanted to know more so badly that they all leaned forward. I knew I had said something important, something so bright it shimmered.

I would rarely talk about it afterwards except with a kind of wild glee. "Burned bad, burned bad," I would say, flying around Playground Number Two in a fury, as if I were running away from imaginary flames. "Burned bad, burned bad. Burned bad, burned bad. My mommy and daddy were burned."

The rest of the morning went fine. I met a few girls that I liked and we had a pretend tea party.

"What do the scars look like?" Linda asked.

"Ugly, like shiny ropes," I said.

"Can I see your mom, please?" another girl asked, her brown eyes pleading.

I said nothing and looked down at the gray sparkles in the floor. After a few awkward moments, we continued our tea party.

That day, Belinda waited outside the school entrance to pick me up. She was a fleshy woman with a round face, her eyes hidden in pillows of fat. She looked annoyed. Some of the tea party girls excitedly looked for my mom, but seemed disappointed when I walked home with

Belinda. We crossed 20th Street in silence. I didn't like Belinda at all. She seemed irritated when Anne and I arrived since it made her job harder, having to pick up after us.

My mother also had a sharp edge to her voice, even though we had just gotten home. The chores seemed endless, and it never seemed like we were doing them right. "Pick up your game. Pick up your toys," echoed throughout the house. Also, my mother kept dropping glasses; each time one crashed to the floor, she would let out a frustrated "Oh, no!" and we would have to stay in our room while my mother or Belinda swept up the small shards of glass.

I was glad to have my big room back, which I shared with Anne, all the books, dolls, and toys in the closet, which I could almost reach without asking. But I missed the country—my aunt, uncle, and cousins; the fields and the fragile mica; Shep and General—and I missed Della. I missed how she spoiled me. I missed her Irish songs.

Here everything was so scheduled—doctor's appointments for my mother and late work shifts for my father. Anne and I were fed early in the kitchen; my mother and father had dinner late at the big dining room table.

That afternoon, I ate with Belinda in the small kitchen, listening to the hum of the refrigerator and opening my sandwich to wipe off some of the peanut butter that overwhelmed the sweet taste of the jam. My mother had disappeared to the bedroom to lie down after her walk from therapy. After lunch, I knocked on her door.

"Can I paint, Mommy?" I asked softly.

"Did you do a good job on your lunch?"

"Yes."

"Okay. Belinda can find the paint set. I'll be up in a while."

I went into the bathroom off my back room, stepped over the pink shag rug and stood on the gray step stool to gaze at my face in the mirror. My light-brown hair curled in ringlets. My eyebrows were nicely shaped, like crescent moons curving gracefully over my round, yellow-flecked brown eyes. My mother had no eyebrows anymore. I thought of that as I lightly touched mine. My eyes were the same size. My mother's weren't; one eye looked as if it were popping out of the socket. At night she wore a gauzy patch over it because it would no longer close. Over the gauze was a piece of Scotch tape that held her eye in place. I wondered if it might spill out if the tape were gone. I then noticed my own cheeks, still slightly red from the country air. My mother had lost her cheeks somewhere on Cape Cod. She had only scars.

Now the surgeons were working on bringing her face back. They were working hard, operation by operation. That's why she had the handle of flesh: the piece of dough that went from the top of her shoulder to her face. It would spread out over her face. That's what it would take to get her face back to normal.

"It will take time, sweetie," my mother said. "We have to be patient."

Now I was changing back into a city girl. I could feel it, a pallor over everything—my school, my cheeks, my house.

Belinda came into the room, heaving a sigh as she

reached high in the closet for the paint set. She put a piece of plastic on the floor as I changed into a T-shirt. Then she left. I sat on the plastic sheet in the middle of my room, alone, and tried to draw birds in the sky. I missed Della, but I knew she was with another family, at least for now.

"Goodnight, Weezie," my mother said after my first day of kindergarten. "I'm glad you had a good day at school. Now get your rest, sweetie."

My mother pushed back my light bangs and stroked my forehead, looking directly at me. I closed my eyes, feeling bad about it, but not wanting to look at her face and be reminded of the fire. Her right hand was stiff like wood.

"Goodnight, Mommy," I said, feeling alone without Annie in the same bed.

"Anne will be here in half an hour. She gets to stay up later now that she's seven."

As soon as my mother left the room, I was terrified and seized by morbid thoughts. Out the window the trees looked like black, burned limbs, though I could see some green buds. I wanted more than anything to get up, go to the living room, and sit with my parents and sister until I fell asleep, curled on the black-and-white-striped couch, hearing my parents' voices and Daddy reading to Annie. Maybe my mom would put her one good arm around me and hold me until I cried. It would be okay that I cried. I felt like crying so much ever since I came home. "There, there," my mother would say softly, "it's okay to cry." But I knew that would never happen.

"Stop making all that noise. That's enough," she would

say. Nothing would change that. That night, I made up a story: General appeared to me—a whine, the thick smell of dog breath, his brown-and-white fur. I felt his heart beating next to mine, faster than my heart. I saw myself lying near the heater, General by my side, so close that his floppy ear was touching my thigh. Suddenly, General became lost to me, and I saw myself floating into inter-minable blackness, trying to find a tunnel that would take me to the light and back to my precious dog. I felt like I was dying, winding down like a record on slow speed; still and fractured like the dead grasshoppers that I'd killed in the fields on the farm. Perhaps they were coming for me, a swarm of tiny bones. Terrified that I would be no more, I counted from one to a hundred again and again until Annie came to bed.

Hours after I fell asleep, I woke up frightened and sat upright in bed for what seemed like hours. I stared at the shadows that covered the rectangular beams in chaotic patterns, beams that were supposed to hold up the house and protect it from danger. Moved as if in a trance out of my bed, I knew I had to get to my parents' room. The hallway was narrow and my arms brushed against the cold plaster walls. The door to their room was half shut, and as I entered, I saw the twin beds pushed together, the wooden headboards touching, and the window with the venetian blinds drawn. I was overwhelmed by the smell. The bandages were wrapped around my mother's right hand and there was a patch of white gauze cover-ing her right eye. But even with the smells, I wanted to crawl in between my parents, to be cradled in the crack in the middle, to be the one who was protected. But I felt ashamed to disturb this sleep of the almost dead. My father was curled up on his side, clutching his pillow, his breathing shallow, like a series of sighs. My mother slept on her back, her arms out of the sheets, covered with scars. The pedicle of flesh from her shoulder to her face was so gruesome I had to turn away.

"Are you still alive?" I whimpered, standing right by my mother's side of the bed.

"Everything's okay, sweetie. Go back to bed."

My mother's eyes closed, but I wanted more. I wanted her to gather me in her one free arm and hold me. But one arm was attached to her face and the other arm was now limp as my mother descended into sleep.

Holding in my tears, sickened by the antiseptic smells, I turned back to where I came from, back through the narrow hallway, my arms brushing the cool walls again, back into my room with Annie grinding her teeth, and back into my bed. I pulled the covers over me and tried to make a cocoon, imagining myself webbed in silk threads, bound and safe. For an hour or two, I stayed awake, my body stiff, counting. Then my eyes began to close and I took in my familiar room—my bed, the walls, the tree outside—and tried very hard not to be afraid. I experienced these nightly episodes repeatedly over the next several months.

Even though what I remember most from that period are the bandages, the Vaseline smells, the nighttime fears, the grief, and the scary changes in my parents, I knew that my mother had filled the closets with toothpaste, Crest for me and Colgate for Anne; she had filled the refrigerator with familiar food and drinks—orange juice, grapefruit juice, milk that still came in glass bottles. People stopped by who I had known all my life. My best friend, Nancy, still lived next door and we walked together to school. I liked the feel of the carpet under my feet, and having my dolls lined up on a shelf above my bed. I liked seeing the picture of me as a baby peeking out from under a white blanket that my mother had framed, so I could see how I'd grown. All these things remained true as life moved on, as I learned to roller-skate down that same serpentine road my mother took to physical therapy, as I learned to ride a bike, as I ate pastel-colored candy buttons off long sheets of white paper, and as I heard the sound of my father's voice—a voice that could have been so easily lost to me.

Chapter Twenty-one

Almost from the first moment my sister saw our mother's face, she swept away the scars into the innermost recesses of her brain, so no one would know that she could see the knotty skin, the abnormal shine, the discoloration that had now lodged itself in tiny crevices—so only she would know about them and not have to broadcast all these scars to the world. Anne had decided that whatever had happened, everything would be fine. It had to be. That's what Mommy wanted. That's what would bring Daddy back. Daddy had always been proud of how smart she was, so Annie set out to do as well in school as she always had and quickly rose to the top of her second-grade class.

At lunchtime on her first day back, friends gathered around her, asking what had happened, why she had been gone for so long. "My parents were in an accident," she said. "Let's play." She climbed to the top of the jungle gym, then monkeyed her way down, laughing with her classmates until the bell rang. During class, she sat in the front row, as close to the teacher as possible. Whenever the teacher asked a question, she shot her arm straight up, knowing she would be picked at least a few times.

She rattled off the right answer and then took a deep breath, feeling proud.

Mrs. Woicek had given the kids a hug before they left the classroom that day. Anne still felt wrapped in her teacher's soft arms as she walked home through Peter Cooper by the chained grass, the playgrounds, down the curvy road to the building, past the blue elevator and up the stairs to 2B. Proudly carrying her key on a lanyard, she opened the door to the apartment. She heard a clanging noise as Belinda was putting away dishes.

"Where's Daddy?" she asked.

"He went out for a while."

"Where's Mommy?"

"Lying down. She's tired."

"Where's Weezie?"

"In the bedroom painting."

Then she knocked on the door to the middle bedroom, where Mommy slept.

"Mommy. I want to go upstairs to Ellen's."

"Hi, Annie. Do you have much homework?"

"Only vocabulary words. I got all of them right yesterday and I know most of them."

"Okay. But change into old clothes and come home by five o'clock."

She rapidly changed into blue jeans and a T-shirt and raced out the door as if she couldn't stand being at home for even ten minutes. When she returned, we ate macaroni and cheese and drank milk for dinner. At the end of the meal, she listened for the elevator and then heard a key turn in the door. She ran to see Daddy, who threw her up in the air and brought her down to the ground. Then he looked tired and sad and went to his room.

Annie felt the burden of everyone's sadness: her sister's for all those months on the farm—the clinging, the nighttime fears, the crying, the constant questions—and now her father's. She was the one who talked to him all the time about books. She was the one who had talked to him most when they went to the Museum of Natural History and stood transfixed before the huge dinosaur. She was the one he talked to most about the stars in the sky, the baseball game, the dazzling lights. I was still a baby then. That's why, on that day in the kitchen in Sherburne, when Aunt Rusty had turned and said Daddy was going to come and pick us up, she had been so excited she could hardly sit still in her chair.

It was Daddy who had read *Charlotte's Web* to her the night before and would read to her again and again and again. Their eyes had teared up at the same time.

> *"Charlotte?" Wilbur said, softly.*
> *"Yes, Wilbur?"*
> *"I don't want to die."*
> *"Of course you don't," said Charlotte in a comforting voice.*

They had read that part last night. Annie was waiting to continue the story, to show her daddy how well she could read. She had trouble with the word "blundered" and planned to ask him what that meant and how to pronounce it. When he went back to his room, shuffling his feet on the carpet, and closed the door to lie down, Annie thought nothing of it. Soon he would come and read to her. But Mommy was the first to get up.

A half hour later, the last bubbles draining out of the tub, Annie dried herself and got into her pajamas. She sat on the left side of the black-and-white tweed couch, waiting for Daddy, anticipating his footsteps, how he would joyfully take his place next to her. Perhaps she would sit on his lap, feel the words wash over her like the waves at the beach as he read, and she would dutifully flip the page: "Now, Daddy?" "Okay, Annie, now."

Tonight, even though Mommy would get mad, Annie wanted to read three more chapters, not just two chapters like they usually did. She would even try to read along with him as she did sometimes, their voices meshing, her voice making his voice higher, lighter.

"When is Daddy getting up?" Annie asked Mommy, who was now walking through the house trying to pick things up with one arm.

"Should be soon. To read. I'll go knock on the door.

"Hank. It's book time. Anne is waiting on the couch."

No answer.

"Hank. It's book time."

"I'm too tired, dear. Tell the children I'll read to them tomorrow. I'm sorry."

Anne, who had been sitting on the striped couch, waiting patiently for Daddy to take his place, saw Mommy walk down the hallway and heard Daddy say he was tired. She began reading out loud to herself, eyes downcast, voice monotone.

"Do you want me to read?" Mommy asked.

"I can read myself," Annie said angrily. "You can read to Weezie."

If it had just been that one particular disappointment, my sister's hurt would have been brief, like a flash of lightning in the sky, something that would strike and then vanish, never to be seen again. But the disappointments had been so long and so deep and so big that the small disappointments, like this one, seemed to weigh on her small body and mind, as if his sadness was her sadness, and the fact that she couldn't pull him out of it, even though they were all home together, was her fault. It was too much for a seven-year-old girl to bear, so she hid herself in book after book to soothe the pain, and to remember how much her father loved to read to her.

From the first moment that my father saw us in the living room of Sherburne and then brought us home on the long train ride, he knew he needed to protect us, care for us, and pull himself out of the depression that was dragging him down into a mental quicksand. He knew he had gotten out of the cellar alive and so had my mother.

"It hurts, Daddy," I would say in a whiny voice whenever my throat was scratchy. "Can you take a look?" I opened my throat wide and thrust out my tongue. My father got a spoon out of the drawer, warmed it on his shirt and put it in my mouth, careful not to put it so far in that I would gag.

Annie sulked if he didn't read to her and seemed lost in books. But things were moving along. From one operation to the next for my mother, a time line of surgeries.

In and out of the hospital: fear, recovery, hope for the final face.

He knew he should go back to work, at least to the fire department. The chief had given him a date when he needed to return, but my father hadn't even called him back, even though he obsessed about money. There was a "sick fund," a term he hated but he was terribly grateful for; friends had all contributed, hundreds and even thousands of dollars. But that money would be gone soon, and he had many bills: two rents, salaries for his secretary at the office and Belinda, the kids, groceries, phone bill, Con Edison bills, clothes and shoes for the whole family.

The lawsuit, which he hoped in a naïve way would quickly be settled, now looked like it could take a year, perhaps even two, before they saw any money. The latest letter, dated April 1, said:

Re: Nayer vs Suburban Propane Gas Corp.

We are enclosing herewith original transcript of examination before trial of Della Duggan. This must be read thoroughly by the witness. If there are any corrections to be made in the testimony and if Miss Duggan does not understand how the correction is to be made, please have her telephone me.

Once the examination is signed, please arrange to mail same to this office in the enclosed self-addressed envelope.

Very truly yours,
Paul Ross

Yes, things were moving along. Yes, Della had been there to let the gas company men into the house on the night of the accident. She had her testimony. She was a witness. Della, now with another family, was of course cooperating, but she would call crying. She was haunted by that night and, without much education, she was insecure and feared the lawyers and any questions they might ask. My mother and Paul Ross had to counsel her, comfort her. It all took so much time and energy. On April 5, another letter had arrived from the lawyers; the postoperative photos had come back.

Enclosed please find postoperative photos of yourself and Mrs. Nayer, which were returned by Mr. Gair's office and are being returned to you in accordance with your request. Copies of the photographs have been made by Mr. Gair.

My father had left the letter on his desk for a few days. Today he opened it. As he read the letter, the photos spilled out, the evidence. He began to wring his hands and went back to his chair in the living room and stared out the window.

They were moving toward a trial, a public trial. He thought of his wife and her gruesome scars. His own scarred hands and face. The pictures, the evidence. The gas company officials on one side of the courtroom, the scarred victims and their lawyer on the other. He knew he had to go through all this, but he just wanted to walk into the sea across the street from their jinxed Cape Cod cottage on a day when he wasn't burned and forget any of this had happened.

"Hank. Stop sitting around all day," my mother said to him one Monday in April. "I'm going to physical therapy. What are you going to do?"

What am I going to do? he thought to himself. What a question! Couldn't she see that he didn't feel well; that his leaden legs anchored him to his rocking chair; that he slept poorly if at all; that Weezie's constant anxiety since she returned was exhausting; that Annie's needs overwhelmed him. And now even she was making demands on him.

"I'm going uptown today. That's what I'm doing!"

"To do what?" she said sarcastically.

"Maybe I'll go to the zoo and watch the seals. They don't seem to have any worries, do they?"

"Oh, dear. Stop being so silly. It's not like I'm asking you to do something unreasonable. Call the fire department. Start setting up the office again and make calls to your patients. Tell them you'll be back next week."

That was Dorothy, he thought to himself. She had it all planned. She had her life planned and his as well. Well, it didn't all work out. He wasn't going to let her push him around.

"I'm going uptown and I don't have to tell you why!"

A few minutes later my mother left for physical therapy. He hadn't walked his children to school like they wanted. Anne had looked back at him longingly.

How could he do this to his children? His heart sank. Waves of guilt washed over him.

He looked at the last letter from Paul Ross again: "Please don't fret over anything about the case. Everything is moving more slowly than we thought, but it is moving along."

Well, he couldn't count on any money from the lawsuit for years to come.

"That money will be gravy," my mother had said in her usual know-it-all tone. "Never count on anything you don't have. Just figure out how you're going to get back to making some money again! It's not as if you have a choice."

He knew she was right, of course. He would have liked to watch the seals, their sleek, black bodies dripping with water, their laughing, inky eyes, their long whiskers. He would take his children to the zoo and they would all laugh. *Look at me. Aren't I cute and fast and funny?* No, he would only think about the seals, but he would actually go up to the office on East 86th Street and climb the tall stairs. He wouldn't tell my mother until it was all set up. A surprise. Plus, he didn't want to give her the satisfaction of always being the one to push him to do things. Being depressed was not something he chose, like what to wear or where to go on vacation. Couldn't she understand? I guess not, he thought.

"I'm going out, Belinda," he said quickly and went out into the sunny April day, wearing a suit coat, shirt and tie, and navy pants. The red Dodge was parked on 23rd Street. He had to keep moving it to avoid tickets. He'd only been in the car briefly over the past months. A few times he had picked up my mother from her operations at Beth Israel on 16th Street, helping his drugged, damaged wife into the front seat of their car and then letting her lean on him as they walked together up to apartment 2B. Today, when he opened the car door, he was struck by the smell of the beach, grains of sand like morsels of memory embedded in the red cushions. After driving in traffic to his office, he reached the garage next door but felt like turning back.

"Hey, doc! It's been months. I heard 'bout . . . "

"Yeah. I know. I'll be here for only an hour or two."

He regretted how curt he was with Fred.

"You have your old space, Dr. Nayer."

My father waved at him then and thought he saw Fred looking at him, taking in the scars, staring.

He walked up the steep stairs to his office and was filled with the familiar smells, a mixture of alcohol, antiseptics, human frailty, and an overwhelming sense of comfort. The long couch was on the right, the table was still stacked with magazines, and there was the large palm plant. This was his office. He was a doctor. This was where he worked, where his patients came to see him, his loyal patients. He wondered how many he had lost to the accident. Two of Davey Davison's, his office partner's patients, were in the waiting room. He walked through quickly, head bowed so no one could see his burned skin, and he found Stephanie, his office assistant, sorting through a stack of papers.

"Dr. Nayer," she said warmly. "I'm so glad you're here. I have so many questions."

"Well, I'm not here for long, but I thought we should go over some things."

What was to be two hours turned into five.

"When are you coming back?" she asked. "About four patients a day, minimum, have been calling." They had heard what had happened. They had sent cards, which flooded the inner office. And months before, just after the accident, so many flowers had arrived. "Take the flowers home," he had told her from the hospital.

"What should I say to the patients?" Stephanie asked, this time more directly than she had in the past weeks. She wondered if she was going to have a job.

"I'll see them. Maybe soon. We'll see."

"Now about Mrs. Feinstein and her heart?"

"Tell her to go to cardiology at Beth Israel. She needs to be seen immediately. Mr. McFarland can wait for a couple of weeks. It's the same problem."

But my father realized he couldn't do this. He couldn't tell someone else to treat his patients. How wrong. How ridiculous. He would have to come back and see them, soon. It had been over nine months. It would be summer again, with all the memories of the past year. He tried to push the horror away and think about his little girls who would run into his arms, even if his arms sometimes collapsed under the weight of too much sadness.

"Listen, Stephanie. I'll be back on Wednesday. Not in the morning. I'm not well in the morning. But after lunch, at one o'clock. You go have your lunch and then come back. We'll sit down and start getting things into motion. I'm tired now. I'll see you Wednesday."

Stephanie, a forty-year-old woman with two children, had grown to love my father over the five years she had worked for him. He was kind, and he took care of a lot of things himself, things other doctors ordered their assistants to do, such as filling out forms and even typing letters, if necessary. If she had to pick up her children or take them to the doctor, he always waved her down the stairs. "Go. There's nothing much left to do," he would say kindly. He never left the office unless all the forms were sent out, everything signed. She came back to a clear desk each morning. She didn't want to lose her position. Now she could breathe a sigh of relief, because he was coming back. Soon the waiting room would be filled. She knew it, even though his patients would be shocked by his pasty skin, mottled from the grafts.

"Oh, Stephanie, go home early today. There's no point in your sticking around." He sounded like an old man.

But would he be up to it? She heard him pad down the steep stairs more slowly than she ever remembered from the past.

"See you tomorrow?" Fred said as he went to get the car out of the garage.

"I'll be back on Wednesday. See you, Fred."

As my father drove home, he thought of what my mother had said the night before. "We can only move on from here. There's no going back to before the accident."

He had wanted to hit something. Smash his fist into the window. See it break. See blood. Instead, he had turned away from her in the bed, so she couldn't see the angry tears that formed in the corners of his eyes.

He was in his usual place in the rocking chair, reading Tolstoy, looking out the window at nothing at all. The phone rang. Belinda answered.

"Dr. Nayer, someone's on the phone. She says it's urgent."

Since both children were out at friends' houses, he grabbed the receiver, although he didn't feel like talking to anyone.

"Dr. Nayer, Mrs. Rosen here," an anxious voice said from the other end. He thought his secretary, Stephanie, might have put her up to it, but he wasn't sure. He felt like hanging up. Didn't she know he had been badly burned? Didn't she know about his wife? That he wasn't taking calls, particularly at home?

"My husband. I think he's having a heart attack. Can you come over? 440 East 23rd Street, 5C."

Her voice—so desperate—moved something in him. Before he could think of the words, he had said them, as if watching himself reach for the doorknob to open a door.

"I'll get my bag and be over right away."

"I'm out for a while, Belinda," he said, grabbing his bag and his coat and rushing out the front door. He didn't wait for the elevator but took the stairs. The walk to the building, another of the red-brick buildings of Peter Cooper, took only three minutes.

"Oh doctor, thank god, thank god," Mrs. Rosen said as she opened the door, tears running down her face.

Instinctively, my father reached up to touch his damaged ear, glad his burned hands were momentarily gloved, and gauged her reaction to his scarred face.

"My burns . . . "

"My husband, Dr. Nayer, my husband." My father walked over to Mr. Rosen, an overweight man sitting in his armchair clutching his chest. Quickly, my father took out his stethoscope and listened for a couple of minutes as Mrs. Rosen pulled her chair next to her husband, clutching his hand.

"Everything sounds fine. Heart is normal. Must be gas. What did you eat today?"

"Thank god, thank god," Mrs. Rosen said, the tension in her face gone, her deep-set brown eyes now glowing.

"I had cabbage soup, a little more than usual, but I often eat it."

His wife leaned over and kissed him on the forehead.

"Mikele," she said, "all is well again."

"Gas pains can be bad," my father said. "They can mimic the sign of a heart attack. It's good you called. I'm sorry about—how I look." He turned his face away.

"I didn't even notice. What's to notice?" she said. "But I'm sorry. I heard about you and your wife. Do you want some tea and dessert?"

"No. I need to get home. The children are returning soon."

"God bless you, Dr. Nayer."

As my father walked down the hallway and pushed the elevator button, he gazed at his burned hands, realizing they were still a doctor's hands. All the years he had spent studying, trying to make his hardworking parents proud, were not lost in that flash fire. He could still feel his children's swollen glands and treat them; he could still hear his patients' hearts with his stethoscope. He hadn't lost all his knowledge. He was still a doctor. He could go back to work.

Chapter Twenty-two

When my father came home with sweetheart roses, my mother seemed taken aback. She had Belinda cut off the stems and put them in a light-green porcelain vase she had bought right after she and my father were married. The flowers looked beautiful on the dark wood coffee table.

That night, my father read a section of *The Merchant of Venice* to Anne and me. "A pound of flesh," he interjected. "Imagine that! A pound of flesh and with no blood!" We were mesmerized by his words, our imaginations working overtime, both of us secretly wondering if our mother's pedicle was a pound of flesh. But we knew to hope that there was blood inside.

After we were put to bed, I can only imagine how my mother and father began their long journey toward intimacy. They had so much to overcome: the scars, the fear, my mother's anger at my father, who, she told me many years later, had "abandoned" her for months when she needed him the most. As much as she tried, she could never understand depression, the dark cave that swallowed my father during that time of trauma and recovery, a depression that followed him for many years.

They must have set out on the slow road back to intimacy moment by moment, just as my mother's persistent voice had reached him, little by little, through the passageway between their hospital rooms.

My parents sat up for some time, across from each other in the black-and-white armchairs, reading. Belinda had cleaned up all the dishes and gone home. The house was quiet; their children were sleeping soundly, at least for the time being. That night, there was a cadence about the air, as if their breaths were in tandem, like they used to be: the end of the day, the quiet time after the storm of the kids, the down time with books, and then the goodnight kisses.

"I'm getting ready for bed," my mother said.

"Me too."

They went into the bedroom and my father helped her take off her shirt and put on her nightgown. He stood closer to her than he had in the past, the scent of sweetheart roses in his mind. When she turned around for him to help her button her nightgown, because her arm was in a sling, he was again struck by the scars that ran down her face, the deep rivulets of damaged flesh. He turned his face away momentarily, breaking the spell. My mother immediately began to talk about the children.

"Weezie had a better day at school," she said, her voice distant.

"It seems so."

"She's not following me around quite so much."

"Yes, things are getting a little better."

With that, my father crawled into bed and let out a brief sigh as my mother put Vaseline on the patch that would cover her eye.

"Are you okay, dear?" he asked. "Can you get the eye patch okay?"

"Yes. I'm fine," she said, relieved that he had finally asked her about herself; that he hadn't moved so far away from her.

"Goodnight, dear," he said.

"Thank you for the lovely flowers."

"I'm glad you liked them."

They both reached over at the same time and turned off their reading lights. My mother lay on her back, as usual, the only position she could sleep in with the pedicle attached from her shoulder to her face. My father curled into his usual fetal position, but this time the sides of their legs touched in the dark.

It had been two months since the last operation. What a great relief! Before this two-month break, my mother had had constant grafting operations of her neck, scalp, eyes, and hands. For each operation she had to be put under anesthesia. For burn patients, anesthesia could sometimes be a problem, as vomiting could affect the skin grafts or lead to an electrolyte imbalance, especially in the beginning. She was given ether and oxygen under a face mask through a catheter. Because she had stopped breathing twice on the table, she was always scared of the anesthesia, terrified that this would be it, that she would never see her husband and children again.

But the grafting needed to be done, one operation after the next—from July to October, October to November, November to December, December to January, January to February, and finally, from March 27th to the 30th. The series of operations started with the pedicle, right before Anne and I returned from the farm. Each time our mother had an operation, she had to be kept immobilized for two weeks so the grafted flesh would attach. An untreated open burn area was compared to a hole in a bucket; everything leaks out: protein, sodium, potassium, calcium, and even red blood cells. She had been treated repeatedly for anemia and infections.

Now we had all been together for almost two months. Annie and I had played with the pedicle of flesh, sometimes smushing it between our fingers to keep it viable. My mother had planned it that way. She wanted her children home with her for a while until she had to leave again for another hospital stay. The last time the pedicle had been formed during the operation and she had her arm in a sling for eight weeks, the skin had died, crushing all hope. But now her children were home and everyone dreamed of her old face, knowing that the scars on her face were temporary, like a Halloween mask. She knew she wouldn't ever look like a Hollywood star, but she was fortunate enough to have the best plastic surgeons in the world working on her face.

The short break from working on my mother was good for Dr. Barsky, her main surgeon, because he was also working on the Hiroshima Maidens, the young women who had been burned by the "great ball of fire" that destroyed the lives of hundreds of thousands of Japanese on that fateful day.

These twenty-five young women were brought out of the shadows of back rooms; some had been hiding away for years. The Reverend Tanimoto had reached out to them by creating a safe haven in the basement of his church, where they could get together and talk about the pain of disfigurement and their hopes for the future. They were young. They deserved a chance at a normal life. Through contacts with America, namely Norman Cousins, and through endless phone calls, political hurdles, and fund-raising efforts, twenty-five women were able to come to America. When asked to be on the team of volunteer plastic surgeons, Doctors Barsky, Hitzig, and Simon had said, "Count me in." They donated hours of their time to help these women. Dr. Barsky would later say that his father had taught him to take care of his family first and then give back to humanity. He had taken care of his family; now it was his turn to give something back.

Most of the women had been burned on the face, neck, and hands, like my mother. They had turned to look up at the fireball and then put their hands in front of their faces when the blast knocked them to the ground. Skin hanging off their bodies, they moved ghostlike to the river where many of their fellow citizens were swept away in the rising waters. Others died asking for water. Many died under buildings. There were so many hurt and so few to help. The Reverend Tanimoto had been one of the lucky ones. He was able to help, to tirelessly bring water, to do what he could. Ashamed that he wasn't hurt when so many others were, he promised himself that he would continue to help heal those who were harmed by the blast.

The twenty-five women were selected after a long and grueling process that turned many others away. They brought with them the hope of their young lives. They wanted boyfriends, children, jobs with design firms, secretarial jobs. They wanted to go on picnics with their families without being sneered at or humiliated. Many of them wore tight stockings over their faces with cutouts for eyes. Barsky had just finished working on three of the maidens when it was time for my mother's next operation.

I pressed my face to the bedroom window, as I did every time she was about to leave for the hospital.

"Don't go away, Mommy," I said, my brown eyes tearing up. "Don't go away!"

"But I have to, sweetie," she replied, "so my face can get all fixed."

We all looked forward to the day my mother's face would be fixed, all better, with the smooth, peachy skin that used to surround her dark eyes. It was the goal, the brass ring. I knew it, wished for it, dreamed of it, hoped for it more than anything. Sometimes at night I dreamed that I couldn't find my mother's face; like a newborn, half blind, I crawled up my mother's body, my infant hands searching for her cheekbones. I always woke up before I could see her. But I knew it was just a "waiting game," as Daddy had said. "We have to be patient."

"Okay, Mommy. But please call me from the hospital."

"I'll call every day after a few days. For the first few days, I won't be able to call, but your grandma and grandpa are coming down from upstate."

"Grandma and Grandpa!" I exclaimed, remembering the butterscotch candy my grandpa always had in his pocket.

On the third Sunday in May, 1955, my mother packed a small suitcase. Annie and I watched her open drawers, pull out changes of underwear for ten days, two bras, slacks, and four large shirts that would be gentle on her skin. We each gave her a lucky penny from our piggy banks, which she put into the zippered pocket of her purse. Just as we finished helping her pack, the doorbell rang. We ran to greet our grandparents, who swept us up in their arms.

"My dear little buttercup," Grandpa said, kissing me on the top of my head while simultaneously pulling out a butterscotch candy and pressing it into my palm.

"Oh Annie, my dear," Grandma said, hugging her tightly and then giving me a hug, too, as Grandpa kissed Annie.

For two weeks my mother was again hospitalized. After the first few days, Anne called her when she got home from school. My mother managed the household from her hospital bed, making sure we did our home-work and that my father checked our math, planning din-ners, deciding whether we could visit friends, telling us what time we should be home, what time we should be in bed.

At the hospital, my mother was taken care of by her favorite nurse, Margaret Jones, who had been with her through all the terrible months and soothed her through the terrifying procedures. Mrs. Jones, who lived with her husband and two children in Stuyvesant Town, the housing development neighboring Peter Cooper, got up a half hour earlier than usual to be with my mother. She made her two children French toast or scrambled eggs, helped them pick out their school outfits, and made sure that they had their homework and workbooks for P.S. 40, the same school that Annie and I attended. Mary, the fifty-year-old crossing guard, would get them safely to school. Margaret then raced down First Avenue, as fast as she could walk, in her white nurse's dress and sturdy oxfords, to be with my mother before her surgery. She never asked her favorite patient if she would like her to come early; she just told her she would be there. Even when my mother had trouble talking and forming coherent sentences, she would always ask Margaret about her children and her husband.

A few times, Margaret was assigned to another floor, and my mother was lonely as she waited on the gurney. Even though there was an orderly who took her up to the operating room, friendly nurses who passed her in the hall, and sometimes a doctor she knew who would say hi, they all moved too quickly. Only Mrs. Jones offered her the steady comfort she needed; only Margaret held her hand down the long ride through the antiseptic halls. Sometimes they would talk as mothers. Before Annie and I came home, my mother confided in Margaret about how she longed for the normalcy of family life, with homework, sibling rivalry, and bedtime stories.

In addition to taking my mother to the operating room, Margaret read her mail and opened packages for her before giving her the required bath or changing her dressings. The difficult task of taking off the dressings and exposing the ailing flesh was lightened for a minute by news from her friends, well-wishers who sent her love and hope through the long days and nights. Margaret had even persuaded the surgeon to allow my mother's loyal nurse friends from the American Nurses Association to feed her. They brought her news of the world of work, a world she had entered so confidently and where she had shone so brightly.

Chapter Twenty-three

A year had passed since the accident and my father was slowly reentering his life. He had started spending three days a week at the office. It was at this time that the fire chief of the New York City Fire Department called with an ultimatum: "Doc, all the men want you back, and only you. But if you're out any longer, we need to hire someone else. Let me know by tomorrow."

My father held the receiver for a minute and stared into space. When he hung up the phone, he remembered that my mother was going to buy him special gloves for the cold. He wondered if she had something to do with all this, but it was a fleeting thought. Five minutes later, he called back and said he would return to work. Within a few days, the forms came in the mail. Sign on the dotted line. Off disability. Back to work. Tuesday nights, every week. Then Tuesdays and Fridays he would be back at Health Insurance Plan, and he'd see a lot of firemen there. He had already gone back to his office. Now he would be on call at night. The fires might be small, out before he got there. He would listen to the firemen's chests, hoping it would be nothing serious, just something to write on the forms. Everything is fine. Everyone can go back to work, he'd say.

But then there would be the other fires—like the A&P fire, the Wanamaker fire, the fire when the plane crashed in Queens—and he'd have to pronounce people dead, see the lifeless bodies and then make sure the firemen were okay. So much to do. So much fire. Flames would shoot out of burning buildings so suddenly; people's lives would be overturned by a candle or an electrical short. Some would die inside, trapped under beds—the most tragic when it was the children. Often pets would come out stiff to sobbing owners. Then, every once in a while, there would be the burns: the horrible, blistering skin, the lasting disfigurement that my father predicted, the fragility of the patients who had to be rushed to the burn unit immediately.

To go to the small kitchen fires, to listen to chests, one after the other—that would all be fine. He would wear his warm gloves. He would probably stay mostly in the fire truck. But to go to the big fires again, to see the flames, to see that horror again, up close. The thought made him shiver, but he looked at the forms. The money was good, necessary, urgent. On his first night back, the Fire Chief picked him up.

"Dear, make sure to take your gloves and scarf—in the front closet." My mother was solicitous, nicer than she had been in a long while. But even with the gloves, he worried about the circulation. So much had been damaged in his hands. If he got frostbite, he could lose a finger, and then where would he be? What was damaged would not come back. He rode in the car in silence, the streets empty except for the rumble of late-night buses going up and down the avenues. The driver hadn't even turned on the alarm because no traffic blocked their path. When they got to the two-alarm fire in Harlem, three engines preceded them. Two firemen had been sent into the apartment where a kerosene lamp had ignited, sending plumes of smoke out through a small window. An elderly woman was the first casualty. She was on a stretcher, and my dad got out of the car.

"I'm Dr. Nayer," he said gently. "What's your name?"

"I'm Mrs. Barnes," she said, coughing. "My cat, Dr. Nayer. I have a cat named General. Can somebody get my cat?" Tears streamed down her wrinkled face as my father listened to her chest, wrapped the blankets tightly around her, and signaled for the ambulance driver to take her to the hospital.

"We'll do everything we can to find your cat," one of the fireman said. "Cats often hide. Once we can get in there, we'll open up all the closet doors."

Mrs. Barnes's eyes had now closed.

"She needs to get moving," my dad said. "Smoke inhalation. Take her to Sinai."

A few minutes later, my father went back to wait inside the car, where the heat was always left on. He rubbed his hands together to keep them warm. Along with the gloves, my mother had gotten him a silk undershirt. He had earmuffs, too. He was grateful that the first person he saw had not been burned, though he knew that smoke inhalation could kill her quickly. Mrs. Barnes would need a lot of good care. He hoped one of the residents wouldn't discharge her too early, which happened a lot. He kept telling the residents that these people with smoke inhalation had to be watched.

When it was the firemen, they usually wanted to jump up the next day and go home to their families. "I'm fine, doc," they would say, and those new residents would think they knew everything. My father got frustrated when they wouldn't check with the attending. Then he would see the firemen come back through the door of Beth Israel, struggling for air, a few of the men never able to return to work because they hadn't been kept still for long enough, hadn't been given enough oxygen, hadn't allowed the damaged lungs to heal. People failed to understand that if the body rests, it can heal itself. Such a simple concept!

A few minutes later, one of the men brought out the lifeless body of a black cat with white feet, the cat who had crouched in the closet, its small mouth open like a fish straining for oxygen. General, my father thought, and turned his face away. Mrs. Barnes could get another cat if she pulled through. For a minute, though, when he saw the body of the cat, he thanked god that his children, his innocent children, had been spared on the night of the fire on Cape Cod.

The rest of the night was uneventful. He was always in awe of the firemen's skills. By the time they broke down the door and poured water all over the apartment, the men who first went up the fire escape had already broken the window to let the smoke out. There was no more smoke inhalation. My father listened to the chests of the firemen, just as he would every week from now on, and gave them the hopeful words: "All clear."

"Goodnight, doc," they all said, one after the other, at almost 3:30 a.m. They would go back to the fire station, then some to their families, others to stay until the next alarm sounded. John, the driver, drove my father downtown to Peter Cooper.

"You know, Dr. Nayer, the men are all glad to have you back. They missed you."

"Oh—I don't believe it. There are plenty of good doctors!"

"No, I mean it, Dr. Nayer. You treat them with respect. They appreciate that. They were really upset about what happened—to you—your wife."

At the word "wife," my father's eyes began to cloud. They spent the rest of the ride in silence.

"Thanks. See you next week," my father said as John dropped him off at 4:00 a.m., right where he had picked him up. There were only a few lights on in the buildings, perhaps one or two insomniacs, he thought. Those with too much on their minds. He put his black bag, coat, gloves, and earmuffs in the hall closet, changed into his pajamas, and lay down next to his wife.

"How did it go?" she asked, lifting her head for a moment.

"Fine, except for an older woman. She lost her cat. She has smoke inhalation. She went to Sinai."

Yes, now he was back in the fray. One night a week at the fire department. Two days a week at Health Insurance Plan. All day on Monday, Wednesday, and Friday at the office on East 86th Street. In the early evenings and on some Saturdays, he would visit his patients in the hospital. Yes, it had all begun again.

After dinner one night, as he sat in his armchair reading, he felt his hands. They had held up, even after all the surgeries. The thumb would always turn in and the scars would never disappear; the yellow skin, thick with scars in some places and mottled red in others, would stay that way forever. But after all the physical therapy, he could hold the stethoscope. He could palpate. He could hold the tongue depressor without it slipping. And now he and his wife were beginning to touch each other again, ever so slowly. Best of all, the children were back at home, back at school, just back.

Chapter Twenty-four

On a warm day in mid-June, my mother decided she would go out and face the world, not just on her circumscribed routes to physical therapy and doctor's appointments, which were now the outline of her life. She wanted to go out to the movies. When my father refused to go with her, she immediately figured out who else might go with her and called her next-door neighbor, Helaine, who would later write to me about her recollections of that night.

"Hank doesn't want to go to the movies with me. Do you want to go? *Love Is a Many-Splendored Thing* is playing at the Gramercy. We can go after dinner. Can Milton watch the girls?"

"I'll call you right back," Helaine said, a small, kind, bright woman who shared my mother's love of sewing. She hung up the phone and broke into tears on her husband's chest, burying her face and sobbing silently so her children, playing Parcheesi in the next room, wouldn't hear her cry.

"What is it?" Milton asked, hugging his wife to him.

"Dorothy. She wants to see a movie with me, looking like she does."

Milton put his hand behind his wife's head and gently rubbed her neck as she cried.

Then she said, "Well, if she's brave enough to face the world, so am I! And I'll feel proud to be with her. That's what I'll feel!" Secretly, though, she felt terrified.

Calling her friend back a few minutes later, Helaine said, "Yes, I'll meet you at eight outside the door."

When they met in the hallway, my mother wore a dark, brimmed hat with an exceptionally heavy veil, which must have been hard to see through, so Helaine walked close to her, their hips almost touching, as they marched to the elevator. When my mother entered the elevator, two women moved to one side and turned their faces away from her and to each other. They must have seen the scars on her hands, and in the blaring light of the elevator, they probably saw not only the scars on her face but also the gruesome way her arm was attached to her face with a piece of flesh. Helaine tried to stare them down. How could they do this to Dorothy, to her friend! One woman looked straight ahead at the door and then practically ran out of the elevator, as if being chased by a monster. Though my mother noticed it all, she chose to think only about the movie, the fact that they were going out. She and Helaine, who must have understood the effect both of the scars and of the pedicle on onlookers, were silent as they walked down the four steps and out to First Avenue, where they hailed a cab. On the way to the theater, my mother saw the cabdriver glancing in the rearview mirror at the way her arm was attached to her face.

At the Gramercy Movie Theater, they found a seat near the back. Helaine warded off stares. My mother breathed a sigh of relief. She was out in the world. When the lights went out, the veil went up. When it did, a couple sitting to her right got up quickly and moved to the aisle so they wouldn't have to see her, even in the dark. Now Helaine was to her left and no one was to her right. The coast was clear.

For the next two hours, my mother's eyes were glued to the screen as *Love Is a Many-Splendored Thing* played. William Holden looked handsome in his brown suit, staring at Jennifer Jones in her light blue dress. My mother admired her blue silk Chinese dress, as well as the orange chiffon dress she wore covered with a shawl. Later, the couple pushed out on a covered boat on the water for the Moon Festival. It was all so romantic, though of course he was a married man. That made it wrong. Still, she liked the romance, the dark clouds covering the moon, and how the couple made noise so the moon would reappear. She liked learning about Chinese culture and some of the superstitions and celebrations.

When Jones, a doctor in a hospital, tended to the little girl, my mother thought of all those months she had longed for her own children. This orphaned child was about Anne's age and needed so much comforting. Then, when the couple embraced by their special tree, my mother forgot the burns and imagined my father looking at her as he always had, as Suyin (Jones) said to Mark Elliott (Holden), "I'm thinking that heaven has prepared for us a great sadness because we have so much." The most romantic moment, though, was when the pair touched cigarettes after swimming in the sea. "You taste of salt," he said.

When the lights came back on, she quickly let the black, lacy material fall down over her scarred face. The millisecond that it took her to lower her veil set off the stares again. And now, of course, people stared at the veil, at her arm raised to her face with the tube of flesh, and sometimes at her hands, though she often hid them inside a coat pocket or under a long shawl.

Now that she was out—really out in the world—she decided she wouldn't look down at the ground so much; instead, she chose to focus her eyes forward on what was ahead. This time, my mother hailed the cab.

"To Peter Cooper," she said. "20th between First and Second." Her voice was commanding, like it used to be. The cab driver didn't even check his rearview mirror. She and Helaine talked about the movie, even humming the song, "Love Is a Many-Splendored Thing." After seeing Jennifer Jones, so gorgeous and fashionable, my mother put the patch on her eye that night without looking at the mirror.

The pedicle was spread over part of my mother's face and she had a few weeks until the next operation. Her arm was no longer raised in the air, at least temporarily, so she began to make her way uptown on the Lexington Avenue bus to Lord & Taylor and Macy's, to get clothes for her two girls, a shirt for her husband, and now a dress for herself. She did this rarely, when she couldn't stand to be stuck inside the house all day.

Though my father refused to go out in public with

her, she was determined, spurred on by her fierce will to face the world and find happiness again. Sometimes she wondered to herself whether her marriage would work, but she always pushed that thought into the very back of her mind. She and Hank were a good match. Everyone said so. They had taken their marriage vows.

Now the children had just started school again, Anne in the third grade and Louise in the first grade. My mother would be hospitalized for almost two weeks, and Belinda, whom the girls didn't really like, hinted that she might go to another family. My mother quickly began making calls, and to her great delight discovered that Della was looking for a new family. What Della had really wanted all along was to return to the Nayers, to her two girls, for whom she had continued to light candles every week when she went to church to sit among the stained glass and incense.

When my mother announced that she was going to the hospital, I began having nightmares again. What if something happened and she never returned? Why wasn't Della back with us? My mother said Della couldn't leave her current family, at least not yet. It would take some time. I didn't like Belinda, but I couldn't show it; I had to be polite because my mother was going to have an operation.

"Dorothy stopped breathing on the table," I heard my father say one day to a friend on the phone. "It was terrifying, but thank god she came back. We worry about it all the time. But we got the best anesthesiologist. He knows the situation backwards and forwards." When I first heard my father say this, I imagined what it would be like if my breathing stopped. I tried to hold my breath, but I hated the suffocating feeling and didn't last very long. Maybe if I had held my breath that day on Cape Cod, really held my breath, my parents would never have been burned.

The night that my mother said she was going away, I held my breath for longer than usual. Then I let the air out in an enormous gasp and looked at the dresser, imagining a red fox. I knew if I cried out, no one would hear me. I also knew my mother would be very mad if I got out of bed. So I waited. Annie came to bed and I still waited. When Annie fell asleep, I still waited. I was waiting up to hear my parents talking. When it was deadly silent, I knew they had gone to bed. They couldn't protect me if they were asleep.

"Mommy," I said, opening the door to their room. "There's a fox behind the dresser. The same fox. He's going to get me."

"Go back to sleep, Louise," she said. "There's no fox."

But after I woke up three more nights in a row, stealing into my parents' bedroom, my brown eyes wet with fear, she went to the Five-and-Ten store on First Avenue and bought fluorescent cutouts of lambs that stuck on the ceiling with thin glue.

"If there was really a fox, he would eat the lambs," she said, while packing her suitcase to go back to Beth Israel Hospital. "Oh, and Della is really going to come back to stay with us. She'll be here in one week. Belinda will leave next Friday."

"Della, Della, Della," I said, jumping up and down in

my mother's bedroom and clapping my hands. "Della's coming back."

Suddenly, I was flooded with memories: Della tying my hair in a high ponytail with a pink satin ribbon, the one with the ridge edges; Della taking us down the steep wooden steps, to the sand across the street on Cape Cod. Della. Cape Cod. I shuddered when I thought of it and pushed the memory away, to make the noise go away, like slamming shut a door to the outside. So many good memories mixed with so many bad ones: sand with fire, earth with burned grass, my parents with me and then gone, completely gone. Would Della still let me lie in her arms? Would Della remember what I liked for breakfast and lunch? Did Della like her other family better?

Belinda left on a Friday, and Della returned on Sunday afternoon, wearing the pink-and-black checked cotton coat she had worn before the fire, her whole being smelling of Lucky Strike cigarettes. My father helped her lug her suitcases back to 4 Peter Cooper Road.

Della had her own scars to deal with, deep pockets of acne that had plagued her since she was fourteen, so I can only imagine what she felt when she saw my mother's facial burns and was thrust into the middle of the mending process for all four of us. She had been there at the beginning of my life, changing my diapers and helping my parents with everything: the house, the dinners, even the vacation on Cape Cod that ended so disastrously. She had become part of the family, counting on my mother's and father's strengths, skills, and education to help her navigate through America.

Anne continued to dislike her, even more now that she was older. I didn't like our room being so cramped again with three beds and Della's clothes in our closet, but I still wanted Della to baby me and secretly counted on her to tie my shoes when I was tired. My mother spent less time with me now that Della was back, and she would also get aggravated if she saw that I was being babied.

"Della is not your maid," my mother said. "You need to pick up after yourself. And stop lying in her lap all the time. You're not a baby anymore."

When my parents paid for Della to have her face sanded, the deep pockets removed, she, too, had her face bandaged in gauze. She spent a couple of weeks healing in our back room, where Anne and I were trying so hard to be normal and wished all the smelly bandages would just unravel and go away forever.

But we were also happy for Della. She felt good, better about herself, more confident. She stood up straighter. She bought some new clothes and spent more time putting on lipstick and looking at herself in our back bathroom mirror. A few times a day, she would just stand there, staring. She wanted a boyfriend; maybe one of the security guards would like her now. Maybe she would have a family, too, someday, although we never found out, because the next time she left she never came back.

Chapter Twenty-five

Around this time, about two years after the accident, Jean Wachtel, my parents' upstairs neighbor, invited them to dinner. It was my parents' first formal invitation after the explosion.

The morning after, once Annie and I had left for school, my mother went to Lord & Taylor, where the smells of the perfume counter overwhelmed her. The small glass bottle of Lancôme was yellow like topaz. The Christian Dior, in a beautiful, hourglass-shaped bottle, smelled like spring, like the month of May when my mother was born. Then there was her favorite, Chanel No. 5, its rich amber color, its musky scent long-lasting in a smart black-and-white case with the classic Chanel logo, two semicircles like horseshoes overlapping. She still had half a bottle of Chanel left from before the Cape, but that smell seemed far away, crowded out by all the other overwhelming smells of the last months: the Vaseline, the pancake makeup that she learned to apply in the hospital, and of course the first awful smells of burns, surgeries, and antiseptics. But today she would begin again with a new bottle of Chanel No. 5.

After her purchase and the constant stares of customers, even of salespeople, she walked briskly to the cosmetics counter where she frequently shopped now. When she saw a woman on duty who knew her, she breathed a sigh of relief. At the Clinique counter, she picked up more pancake makeup and some lotion in a pretty, light-green bottle with a silver top that was hard for her to open. She always had to ask someone to loosen all the tops for her, but she loved the way the name Clinique was handsomely printed across the glass bottles.

My mother had never used much makeup in the past, only a little blush and some Vaseline. Part of it was frugality. Why spend money on fancy lotions if Vaseline worked as well? It always had for her; Vaseline plus luck. She hadn't spent oodles of money on foundation, makeup remover, toner, eye makeup, all with names like "intensive night cream," "moisture surge," "deep cleansing," "deep comfort." All the silly names, she thought, just too much.

After she purchased some foundation from Mary, who had helped her many times before, she went over to the lipstick counter. Lipstick was especially important for her, as her lips had been burned off. She literally had to draw them on and try not to let the moisture from her mouth constantly smudge her lipstick and leave her looking like a complete mess. The outside of her lips looked like the inside of most people's lips, that shiny, wet part that is usually hidden. She had trouble keeping her lipstick on. She didn't want to look like a floozy with ruby red or electric red, but some of the colors, like coffee or russet, were too dim. She needed some pizzazz, so people could actually see she had lips. She picked a coral color, bright but sophisticated, and then went over to the silk scarves.

That day, even though it was hot, she wore a thin, white cotton scarf wrapped around her scarred neck, secured with a silver brooch. She looked at the scarves hanging like dripping icicles from hangers: geometric patterns, paisley prints, deep greens and yellows and oranges, just right for the spring and summer, just around the corner.

She knew what she wanted: a dress for the party, a dress that might call her husband to her again. She wondered if such a dress existed, if they were bound to lie apart in their twin beds filled with memories: their first meeting at Columbia, and all the memories of New York. She remembered Texas, where Hank had been stationed before he shipped out in August 1942, a month after they had discovered the joys of married life. Then his departure, so far away and for so long, her deep longing to have children, her fear that he might die overseas. She had written to him every day. As she smelled the lilac scent at the perfume counter, she thought of her husband for a minute as she used to think of him in the first years of their romance, how she listened for news of the war, news of Persia, imagining him imagining her.

Now, night after night, as she lay in bed next to her husband, she wondered if he, too, thought about her in that way. Sometimes she felt the old feeling, but then he would turn away. He always turned away.

She knew she couldn't pick a low-cut dress because of her neck.

"At least your breasts and body weren't burned," her mother had said, with unsettling anguish in her face as she looked at her only daughter, her Dotty, the forever-mangled face of her baby girl. Yes, at least her breasts weren't burned.

Forty years after the accident, my mother stayed with me in my Haight-Ashbury apartment and said, "Look how my breasts don't sag." I dismissed her comment at the time, in one of the many moments of our mother-daughter disconnection, not understanding her need for some part of her womanhood to be salvaged, pure, unmarred.

For the party at Jean's, my mother needed a scarf, something shimmery, something shiny, anything to take peoples' eyes away from her scarred face and down to her glittery covering, like the long, silver tail of a mermaid in a children's book.

That evening, she put on a silver, glittering long-sleeved dress and wore a lavender scarf around her neck. She had on her Chanel perfume, and her fingernails were painted a light pink. She had found black patent-leather shoes and a purse to match. My father dressed slowly that night, laboriously putting on his pants, a white shirt, a navy tie, and a tweed sports coat.

"I'm not so sure I'm up for this," he said to my mother, who silently held back tears. "I'm not really up for much socializing, you know."

She didn't answer him. He was seldom up for much, even before they were burned. She'd had to drag him to places. Once he got there he'd probably cheer up, she thought, as she put on her black pumps, drew on her lips with her new lipstick, and placed a monogrammed hand-kerchief in her purse. Della was already in the living room watching us play dress up, Annie wearing a long, white silk slip and high heels, and I in a pink slip, which I had up around my neck. We were both searching through the wicker dress-up hamper for high heels and pulling out black ballet slippers.

"Mommy, where are you going? How long will you be gone? Can I call you?" I asked anxiously, turning away from the hamper and seeing my parents about to go out the door.

"We're just going upstairs, to the Wachtels'. To Amy's house. We'll be home in a few hours, but you might be asleep."

"I'm waiting up," Annie said.

"Me, too. I'm waiting up."

"You both need your rest, and listen to Della."

"Bye girls," my father said. "We'll be home soon."

Soon. Why did he say soon! What a stick-in-the-mud, my mother thought to herself, smoothing her dress, now wrinkled slightly around her belly, which was flattened by the new white panty girdle she had bought that afternoon.

When my mother pushed the elevator button to go to the Wachtels' apartment, my father imagined the four of them eating dinner, the Wachtels' daughter, Amy, probably in the back room about to go to sleep. They would have read bedtime stories to her already. He would stay for an hour or so; that would be more than enough. He wanted to go home, finish the Hemingway book he was reading, and go to bed. He had some patients to see early the next morning.

When Jean opened the door, my father saw a sea of people milling inside. This was a complete surprise. Not just Jean and Sandy, but four other couples, some people he didn't even recognize. He sucked in his breath, horrified. So many people seeing him and his wife like that. All their burns. All the questions. His face tightened with anger. He wanted to bolt.

"Hi, I'm Dorothy Nayer," my mother said, waltzing into the room. "I'm Dorothy Nayer," she kept repeating, learning the names of two new couples from the building as she continued walking to the back bedroom, where she placed her purse. She left my father still standing near the doorway, though inching closer and closer to the living room couch, where he managed to find a seat next to Sandy, the host. For a minute he surveyed the room, watching people watching him and my mother. My mother had so disarmed everyone with her directness that only a few people kept furtively staring at her face. Soon everyone was engaged in conversation; and the scars receded. The voices, the eyes, and the expressions took over.

My parents were one of the last couples to leave the party that night, my mother basking in her newfound freedom, going to a special event, talking with other couples. My father held court on the couch in his usual intellectual stance—reciting a line or two from Shakespeare—"a tale told by an idiot, full of sound and fury, signifying nothing"—then quickly transitioning to the dirty politics of Joseph McCarthy and the culture of fear—"I can't believe anyone takes that guy seriously. And all the lives he's ruined!" Then he answered the usual questions that people ask doctors: about the polio vaccine for their children; whether the swimming pool on 20th Street was safe; the name of a good pediatrician.

When my father, still slightly inebriated from two martinis, turned the key in the door to our apartment, my mother stood close to him. Her perfume filled the air of the long hallway, the hallway that only four hours ago had been filled with dinnertime smells, pot roast, carrots, mashed potatoes, spaghetti and tomato sauce. My father held the door open as my mother brushed by him, her lavender silk scarf caressing his cheek.

When the door closed behind them, they knew. The children were asleep, the door to their room tightly closed. Two years had now passed. They had gone to a party together. My mother had on her new dress.

My mother walked down the hallway with my father following close behind. Even if she turned around in all her silk, her rose perfume, and her scars, nothing would deter them. My mother hastily glanced in the mirror and decided that tonight she would not take off her makeup. So what if the pillowcase got dirty. She'd leave it on over the lobster-red part of her face, which was only covered by a thin layer of skin. The thicker layer would come soon, within a year or two, she didn't know anymore. Tonight she didn't reach for her white gauze patch, her Scotch tape, or her Vaseline with its thick, oily smell. She dabbed some more rose perfume behind her ears and on her wrists. For a second she stared at the white scars that covered her hands like tributaries.

When she came out of the bathroom, her light-green negligee exposing part of her breasts, those pure, unscathed breasts, my father must have been waiting as one who had been trying for so long to remember and to forget. The air was thick with the scent of perfume and the window was slightly open under the venetian blinds. At that moment, they inhabited a silence that seemed reserved for only the two of them. They put their arms around each other as my father moved his body next to hers on the bed—the same bed where they had cried out in their pristine sterility, the bed that had housed only the injured, the burned, the damaged.

At first they were hesitant, but they both knew any hesitation would be deadly. Then everything fit together and the old feelings of love, life, and sensuality consumed them both in the perfect darkness. They made love.

Later, my mother went to the bathroom to place the gauze patch over her eye. When she looked at her face in the mirror, she saw that her eyes were shining, like they had on the day that her children returned.

The week before Anne started fourth grade, she organized everything: six pencils; a thick, navy spiral notebook with wide-lined paper for notes; and, this year, dividers—blue, green, red, and yellow ones for each subject. The weekend before school started, using her neatest handwriting, she wrote "Science," "Math," "English," and "Social Studies" on the tabs and then pushed them into the clear plastic. She also got Mom to buy her a set of colored markers, which she loved using to doodle on the fronts of her notebooks or in between her class notes. She drew flowers, yellow daffodils waving in the wind, like in the poem "Daffodils" by Wordsworth, which Daddy would recite at the dinner table. "When all at once I saw a crowd, / A host, of golden daffodils," he said. Other times, she tried to draw faces, but she had trouble getting the nose where it should be, and the eyes drooped. She never tried to draw Mommy's face, though everyone promised it would change. She hoped it would change soon, because she felt embarrassed when she walked down the street with her and everyone stared at the way the skin seemed to be pasted onto her mom's cheeks and at the hairless, penciled eyebrows.

Mrs. Goldstein, her fourth-grade teacher, was enthralled by Anne's bright and spunky personality. "Anne, would you please read that passage out loud from *Stuart Little*?" she said in the second week of school.

Anne read and the room was silent:

When Mrs. Frederick C. Little's second son arrived, everybody noticed that he was not much bigger than a mouse. The truth of the matter was, the baby looked very much like a mouse in every way. He was only about two inches high; and he had a mouse's sharp nose, a mouse's tail, a mouse's whiskers, and the pleasant, shy manner of a mouse.

She read with Daddy's intonations, a dramatic voice that went up and down with the syllables—a hypnotic voice. Like Daddy, she thrilled at the lines.

The rest of the day was taken up with math and science. In math class, they were going over more complex multiplication, like 121 × 8 or 732 × 3. They also had word problems, which Daddy loved to help her with: A bottle of sudsy shampoo contains 12 fluid ounces. If there are three bottles, how many fluid ounces of sudsy shampoo are there in the three bottles combined? "Easy!" she would say, and they would quickly figure it out together. "If you think about it," he said one night, "everything is numbers. That's the beauty of numbers!"

After school, she and Anne Davis went to Molly's on First Avenue and bought vanilla egg creams with their allowance. Mom let her go to Molly's two days a week, as long as she came right home afterward and did her homework. But Annie liked to save her homework for after dinner. When she came home that day, she said hello to Mom and marched back to her room, put her book bag on her bed, lay on the neatly pressed sheets, and opened up her fourteenth Nancy Drew book. Anne was reading about three Nancy Drew books a week, knowing when this series was over, she would read all of Sue Barton. Then she would read the Cherry Ames Nurse series. She had already read all of The Bobbsey Twins.

"Anne, don't you think you should begin your homework?"

"Later, Mom. I'm reading."

"Well, start it sooner rather than later. I don't want you up past your bedtime!"

"I won't, Mommy," she said angrily, burying her face further into the book. "Can't you see I'm reading!"

"Anne, never talk to me in that tone of voice!" Then Mom said, "I'll be back in a few minutes. I'm going down to get the mail."

As soon as she left the house, Anne ran into our parents' bedroom, found Mom's stash of M&M's in the bottom dresser drawer, and gently took the rubber band off the black package so it wouldn't break. When the rubber band broke anyway, she searched frantically in our mother's desk drawer for another one before Mom came back. Luckily for Anne, Mom took longer than usual to get the mail that day.

For a while now, Anne had secretly been taking Mommy's stash of candy from her dresser and climbing onto chairs to grab three or four chocolates or cookies out of the kitchen cupboards. She only took little bits at a time, but she had started to put on weight.

Anne now counted out five M&Ms—not enough for Mom to realize any were gone, but enough to satiate her craving for the crunch of the colored shells and the smooth chocolate on her tongue. Then, as always, she washed her hands before Mom appeared with the mail, lay back down on her twin bed, and picked up the Nancy Drew book where she'd left off.

After Daddy ate, she would do her homework. She would do it when she wanted to, not when Mom asked her to. If she had a question, Daddy could answer it. He knew poetry. He could even recite lines in Latin or German, and sometimes in French. He often said "Voilà" and "Au revoir." He knew history. He talked endlessly about the mighty Arno in Florence, about the fall of the Roman Empire, about John Wilkes Booth just before he shot Abraham Lincoln. He recited lines from Shakespeare. Sometimes, when she went to sleep, he would say, "Good night, sweet prince, or princess I should say," or he would call from the doorway, "May flights of angels sing thee to thy rest!"

After his dinner, Daddy would be all hers—at least when she had homework to do. Over the past months, he had spent more time with her. That year, they bought the *World Book Encyclopedia*, a big, white set of books. When she had to do a report on the green frog, he was happy to get the F book off the shelf and flip to the frog page. They looked at the pictures together and Daddy helped her read. "Frogs are amphibians," he read. "*Amphi*— means 'both' and *bios* means 'life'. They have strong hind legs and absorb water through their skin, so they never have to drink. Some interesting facts: the cricket frog can leap forty times its length in one jump." Anne remembered visiting her grandparents in upstate New York one time when Grandma had a pool with tadpoles. If they had stayed only a week longer, they would have seen the tadpoles change into frogs. They did see what looked like possible eyes. Daddy could talk for a long time about the tadpoles, the science of it, the mystery of it.

So that's why Anne waited to do her homework. She would have Daddy all to herself.

Chapter Twenty-six

My mother was determined to be the same person after the accident as she was before. She threw herself into working with fabric and patterns with the dedication of an artist. Silky maroon blouses and handsome camel skirts came alive under her hands. Few people knew the determination it took for her to hold and thread a needle. Sometimes she would rest the needles in her mouth, and I remember my father getting angry, afraid they would slip into her throat, since her lips no longer had structure where the tiny pins were precariously perched. As she sewed, she devised new ways to cover the scars on her neck, designing high collars and silky scarves to match her blouses. As her wardrobe grew, she began to believe that perhaps she could work again.

Three years after she was burned, the call came from Shirley Fondiller at the American Nurses Association. They needed a grant writer. My mother felt momentarily sick to her stomach, like the time she looked at herself in the mirror for the first time at Beth Israel Hospital. How would she manage to be in an office, where everyone would see her? How about the people who had known her before? But she was also thrilled.

She had never looked for a job in her life; she had always been sought after. Now, even with her burned face and all that had happened, she could still go back to work. Her spirits rose.

"When you're finished, you can either come to the office or we can have a courier pick it up," Shirley said.

"I'll deliver the material," my mother replied.

Two days later, a package arrived in the mail. She handled it gingerly at first, as if it might break. Then she opened it and saw the work she had to do: get money for student nurses to travel to different hospitals so that they could shadow nurses and keep up-to-date on treatments for heart patients. There would need to be a supervisor, too. Maybe my mother could even write herself in. That might be going too far, she thought. How would she be ready to travel to different hospitals? But maybe, just maybe.

Then she sat in her red-and-black armchair and cried. Images of herself graduating second in her class from Columbia's Teachers College paraded before her eyes, as did memories of teaching at the University of Michigan. She missed that world, her world, and she missed her old face and old hands.

The night before the delivery, she went into her closet and looked at her clothes. She found a black herringbone suit, checked it for stains, and then found a white linen shirt. The top drawer of her closet dresser was now filled with scarves of all colors. She picked out a long, white scarf, one that would wrap securely around her neck; she found camel cashmere gloves that would match her camel coat. The gloves would cover her hands well. She would, of course, wear a panty girdle, stockings, and her black shoes. The makeup would take a long time to put on, the pancake base, the eyebrows neatly penciled in, most importantly the lipstick, and then her hair; she would make sure to leave enough time to get ready.

If she left Peter Cooper at 11:45, walked to First Avenue, and waited for the bus, she should easily get up to 59th Street at 12:30. If the bus came right away, she might be early. She didn't want to be early, though. Most of the people in the office would be gone at 12:30—off to luncheon places, having shrimp salad, perhaps a glass of white wine, talking shop, a life she could only imagine returning to. But this was the first step, a baby step. She hoped she wouldn't see many people. She would go out in the world, get on the bus, and ward off the stares, but she wasn't prepared to answer questions and talk about the accident.

The walk through Peter Cooper was uneventful. Even the women sitting on the benches who used to gossip hardly noticed her walking by them. She felt good in her work suit, her camel coat, her nylon stockings. She could look down at her shoes and see the handsome silver clasps. She carried a light leather briefcase that she had bought before she began teaching. That briefcase had held many important papers, teaching materials, student lesson plans, and grant proposals, reflecting the ways that she wanted to change the field of nursing. Yes, she felt good.

But leaving Peter Cooper was another matter. Taking the bus was terribly upsetting. In crowded, small places, even the walls seemed to stare. She could see people waiting for the perfect moment, when she would turn her face again, to gawk. She wouldn't give them that satisfaction: she stared out the window at Manhattan's second-story city, all the stores that you could only see from high up on a bus.

After months of warding off the questions of children, she now welcomed their directness. Some asked why she had a clown face. Once, when she was wearing a patch, a child asked her if she was a pirate. Instead of being annoyed, she loved their innocence. Children were fascinated by the round goose bumps that miraculously appeared on her face in the winter, since the skin had been grafted from her stomach. Skin keeps its properties wherever it is transferred. But now: it was the furtive stares that unnerved her, the way people looked at her and then turned away, sometimes covering their mouths as if she could infect them with her scars.

She walked through the glass doors of the American Nurses Association and breathed in the scent of work, taking in the energy of busy people walking with determination. Now she had a place to go to. She, like her husband, had worked hard to get where she was: at the top of her field. She wasn't going to let this accident deter her.

Just as she was starting to feel better, three people walking by abruptly lowered their faces when they saw her. Losing steam, she wanted to be home in Peter Cooper, in her little apartment, in her little world where only her family and her neighbors would see her. But she straightened up, remembering the years of walking with books on her head for her posture, pulled her scarf a little further up around her neck, and walked into the elevator. Thankfully, no one was there. She had timed it right.

When the elevator doors opened, she felt a fluttering in her stomach as she recalled the sound of the doors opening and letting her children come back to her, that day in late March. But this door opened to another part of her life: her work life. Holding her briefcase in her gloved hands, she unzipped the side pocket and quickly took out the manuscript. She didn't want to give the receptionist a chance to stare at her. Again, everything went well, so easily. Hardly anyone was around. The receptionist, a twenty-something young woman, was talking on the phone, engrossed in a conversation, and had little time to engage my mother or stare at her face.

"You have something to leave?"

"I'm Dorothy Nayer. I have a manuscript." The young woman faced her for a moment and then turned her face away. By this time my mother was used to the sudden turning away and now kept her gaze on whoever was trying to avoid her. It seemed to work.

"Oh. Shirley mentioned you might drop by. She's at lunch. I'll hand it to her."

With that, the young woman went back in earnest to her phone conversation. If the receptionist whispered or said something about the burned lady, my mother didn't care and didn't hear it. She felt lighter, as if she had sprouted new wings. She was back in the world of work. After more operations, when the skin on her face would be baby-smooth, when she looked good and didn't need the wide scarf anymore, she would go back to work. She would go out to lunch with the others and have her shrimp cocktail, maybe even a glass of white wine, and she and her colleagues would share a dessert like schoolgirls, dipping their spoons into something sweet. Life was moving on. Family life first and now her work life. She would feel the excitement and not pay attention to the stares. Nobody, nobody at all, would make her feel bad. She wouldn't let them. When she got back on the bus, she thought of a million things she needed to do. With work and the girls and managing the household, life would be busy, very busy, again.

Two weeks before our August vacation on Long Island, my mother let Della go.

"The girls are too old now," my mother had said, looking directly at Della, who held her head a little higher ever since her face was sanded.

Having held the girls since they were babies, lived through the trauma of the fire, and returned to "her family," Della never expected she would have to leave. She thought she had a place with them forever.

"The children can manage by themselves. We'll write you a great recommendation and give you money for a few months at least."

Della turned her face away from my mother and started crying.

"This has nothing to do with anything you've done," my mother said, softening her tone. "It's just the time has come. The girls need to spread out more in the room. I'm sure you'll find another family easily."

Della asked to be excused and went back into the bedroom. My mother could hear her crying.

That night, Anne and I were told Della would leave soon. Anne was happy and started thinking about how she could spread out her toys, books, and records in the area Della inhabited. My mother talked about getting screen doors to separate my part of the room from Annie's. Annie couldn't wait for that to happen. I was worried about losing Della again, but I tried to be a big girl.

A few days later, Della left, angry that she had to leave the only home she knew away from Ireland. There were no big good-byes or celebratory dinners or emotional outbursts. She wanted to leave when no one was around. She said she'd keep in touch, but she never even said good-bye to Annie or me, never called, and never even wrote us a letter. She must have been devastated that my mother didn't need her any more.

She had money to go to the Young Women's Christian Association, where she would live again until she found a new situation. She had no boyfriend, no children. We never even saw her at Peter Cooper again. Maybe she married; maybe she found a way to go back to Ireland; maybe she disappeared into another family's day-to-day life in New York City. Now she must be an old woman. I wonder if she thinks of all of us as I still think of her.

That August, we rented a house in Sag Harbor. I pointed out the apples and pears on the trees in the garden, determined to share my delight with Anne. She was trying not to stumble up the front steps as she carried a game of checkers, her stuffed snake that Daddy had bought her during one of Mommy's hospital stays, and a canteen for lemonade.

"Look inside!" she called back.

The dining room was graced with a huge wooden cabinet covered with mirrors—mirrors wide enough for three people to see themselves fully—and almost half as tall as the ceiling.

"You girls have a choice of rooms," Mom said, showing us the bedroom downstairs and the attic on the third floor.

"I want the attic," Anne said, falling in love with the upstairs room with round windows and endless privacy. I was happy to have the bedroom near my parents.

"Daddy said he'll take us to the beach tomorrow," I said to Anne.

"I know."

"Daddy said they might not have sand crabs, though."

"Louise. Time for bed," Mommy called out. I got into my pajamas and sat on the couch while Daddy read from *The Wizard of Oz*. I saw the swirling tornado funneling through the sky as Dorothy ran after Toto in the blackened landscape. I imagined Dorothy's house being sucked away and swept thousands of miles to the land of Oz. I knew the scarecrow would later be set on fire; the evil, winged monkeys would capture the four travelers and lock them in the wicked witch's castle. Imagining her sickly green, ugly face, I shivered and rested my head on my dad's chest.

That summer at Sag Harbor and forever after, my mother couldn't come to the beach. Even when she sat under a beach umbrella, the sun seared her skin. She couldn't sweat because of her grafts, so the heat was unbearable for her. She stayed home while my father took us to Westhampton Beach and taught us how to jump waves beyond the breakers. We stayed in the water for what seemed like hours, riding the waves, our bodies coated with salt water, seaweed encircling our ankles.

At the house, Anne and I would monkey up trees, our muscled bodies tasty with sea salt. Anne lost the fat she'd gained from all the stolen candy. We went out for pizza in town and played cards and checkers at home at the long dining room table next to the mirrored cabinet. Sometimes my mother, who loved to go on adventures, would put Anne and me into the car and say, "Let's get lost." We would drive up and down small country roads, listening to dogs bark at the roar of the engine, interrupting the still- ness of the air, and watching bugs veer toward the car like kamikaze pilots disintegrating into the windshield.

One night at Sag Harbor, under a threatening sky, we sat down to a spaghetti dinner. Mommy often broke into awful coughing fits, set off by a constricted windpipe from her surgeries. She would take a bite and begin to choke, a breathless kind of choking that made the whole table silent. Then suddenly, Daddy, unable to stand the sound of his wife choking, would demand that she drink some water, demand that the choking stop. In the only voice she could muster up at the moment, she would argue with him. This would go on for a few minutes. After din- ner, Daddy got out a bowl of pretzels and Mommy made popcorn, and we all sat together in the living room in front of the TV, watching Jack Benny.

All too soon, it was time for bed. As I got into my pajamas, I saw lightning crack the sky, a luminescent Z in the darkness. The sound of thunder flooded the house as rain pounded the roof and windows. I asked to stay up a little later, not wanting to be alone during the storm. My eyes grew weary, though, as I read my Bobbsey Twins book, so I soon crawled into bed. Later, I heard Anne climbing the stairs to her attic room.

In the middle of the night, I heard my mother's voice: "I want Anne out of that attic. I don't want her up there. The way the wind is blowing, the salt spray and the curtains—it's too much like the Cape."

My father didn't reply, but I heard his footsteps on the stairs, and then Anne's voice: "What is it, Diddy? It's dark outside."

Then my mother rushed into my room and woke me. "Get up, sweetie, get up right now. I want you to come with me."

I rolled sleepily out of bed and held onto my mother's hand as she led me to the dining room table. She sat with her back to the mirrors and I sat next to her, my head in her lap. Anne and Daddy sat across from us.

"I just wanted us all together," she said.

Anne and I were quiet but glanced at each other across the wooden table. My father looked sadder than he had looked in months. The rain was pounding on the roof, a hard kind of pounding. The lightning and thunder had disappeared. We were all safely inside.

Outside, the fruit trees would be drinking in the cool, fresh rainwater. Everything was growing in the perfect ritual of summer. It was August and everything was blooming. Mother had once been beautiful, with light-brown hair and ivory skin, her dark eyes bright as jewels. Now we were a new family.

Chapter Twenty-seven

A friend of mine was mugged while walking out of his house on Kansas Street. He suddenly became agoraphobic—afraid of the streets, afraid of the world, and afraid of the dark. A hypnotist, Isabel Gilbert, was recommended to him. She made him a personalized tape after asking for his life story and the reasons he had sought her out. His rapid recovery as he navigated through the dark streets, and his ability to hypnotize himself, inspired me to see her. Nina was helping me week by week, but my hands still shook when I went over the bridge. My body, still not my own, was sometimes taken over by a force I had to reckon with. I wanted all the help I could get.

I clutched the steering wheel too hard as I drove to Isabel's Marin County senior residence, an unlikely place for a hypnotist. I should, I thought, be going to a woodsy house teaming with tabby cats, New Age music in the background. Instead, I arrived at a pristine residence, walked down the hallway, past the frail and elderly in wheelchairs and walkers, to Isabel's apartment and rang the bell. I was still reeling from the ride and tried to deep breathe.

It took her a while to open the door. Her eyesight was not good, though she could still read. She had long hair pulled back and wore comfortable pants and a plaid shirt. Her apartment was cluttered. Books and piles of papers stacked at least a couple of feet high sat on the dining room table. Pictures of her grandchildren rested in wooden frames on the piano.

"I didn't want to move to a senior residence," she said. "I went into a depression the first day I arrived because of all the old people. I missed my home. But I had to move since my eyes have been failing. The best solution was to hypnotize myself. The suggestion was: I will be very happy here. I practiced at least three times a day. Now I'm fine. I like it here and I have friends. It took me exactly two days to get over the depression."

Case closed, I thought. Life can be as easy as that. Just turn a switch and tell yourself to be happy. After bringing me a glass of water and sitting me down in a comfortable recliner, which moved me back almost to a sleeping position, she briefly went over the tapes she had made for me after reading my story. "I have given you a suggestion." She played the tape.

"As I let go of my negative past, I turn my life around, handling my life with a new inner calm as I live my life, one day at a time in the here and now."

"Do you like it?"

"That's sounds fine," I said, not really knowing what makes a good suggestion, the cynical New Yorker battling with my desire to be hypnotized out of my panic.

She pulled up a chair next to me and her voice became monotone and soothing. "Now I'm going to hypnotize you, and I want you to breathe deeply." She put her hand on my stomach and chided me for taking such short, shallow breaths. Then she suggested that I eat regularly for my blood sugar and stay away from sweets. "Diet can help a lot with panic attacks," she said. "Okay. Now relax and listen to my voice."

She put a black-and-white picture of a vortex in front of me and told me to focus on it, keeping my eyes open. I managed to get into a relaxed state in a very short time. My breath got deeper. My limbs felt like jelly. For a minute I was afraid that my arm might be paralyzed.

"You can always move your limbs if you want to," she said, as if anticipating my feelings. "Poets and artists make good subjects," I heard her say. "Relax the eyes, drop the jaw. Your lids are getting heavy."

Then I was to see a skywriter writing numbers in the sky. "100. Let that number go. 99. Let that number go." Amazingly, I was almost sleeping, entranced by the number-clouds fading into the blue sky. Only half an hour before, I had been panicking on a crowded California freeway.

I could hardly feel my body. I felt like I was floating—a pleasant sensation. She told me there were piles of leaves, my negative past, that needed to be burned. I imagined the leaves burning, turning to ashes. She led me through the accident and out the other end, telling me that I no longer needed to be that terrified child. For a number of minutes I must have been in a deep hypnotic state, hearing her voice which sometimes rose to a high-pitched tone and then went down deep, the vibrations helping me absorb the suggestions into my brain. I know

I sobbed at one point; when I woke up, my shirt was wet from my tears.

"You'll be okay," she said. "You have a full life and can now let go of the past."

I was to hypnotize myself at least a few times a day, by imagining a beautiful place in nature. "Your ears are tuned into the sounds, even the silence. Your nostrils remember the smell of the air. Let go. Let go completely. The wave of relaxation flows down the body to the tip of your toes." As the tape went on, she said, "Most of the things people worry about never happen."

Every night, before sleep, I was to imagine the burning Cape Cod house and rescue myself, the four-year-old child. I was to hold her in my arms and tell her, "You're safe, you're loved, you're healthy."

I held my tapes in a white plastic bag and said goodbye to Isabel, who told me to call her if I had any questions. She had not only made me two tapes but had told me how to do self-hypnosis for three minutes. "I have some patients who say they don't have three extra minutes in the day. Can you imagine?"

I got on the freeway feeling much calmer, but still clutching the wheel. I continued to take baths upon coming home, to soothe my nerves—but the tapes were a godsend. I listened to them when I wasn't working or watching the children. Sometimes I played the tapes three or four times a day. At the College of San Mateo, when I had a break between teaching classes, I went into a small room with a lock and lay down on a couch. There I hypnotized myself, giving myself the suggestion that I would make it home safely, that I would be relaxed on

the freeway. After a couple of weeks of constantly listening to the tapes and two or three self-hypnosis sessions
a day, I stopped clutching the wheel so hard on the way
home from work. Between Nina and self-hypnosis, I was
beginning to heal. In a few weeks I would drive to Lake
Temescal in the East Bay and back across the Bay Bridge,
the fear only a slight fluttering like a bird's feathery wings.
Yes, I was healing.

*

Dear Dorothy and Hank,

I do hope that you and the children are well.

*This is in the nature of a report to you, based upon
communication which we received from the Boston
attorneys in response to our request for information as
to the progress of the case.*

*Suits are pending in the Federal and State Courts
against H. W. Snow & Sons, Suburban Propane
Utility Gas Co. of Rhode Island, Suburban Propane
Gas Corporation, and Phillips Petroleum. They state in
their letter as follows:*

*"Preparation of this case has and continues to receive
high priority in this office."*

*They expect to take depositions here in New York
within the next five or six weeks and that probably
means that you will be questioned by the attorneys for
the defendants. In advance of the date set, we will
arrange conferences to discuss the matter.*

*In the meantime, we have been informed that the
case has not yet appeared on the trial list. That means
in effect that the case has not yet been set down for*

specific term for trial. But we have the assurances of the trial counsel, Mr. Schneider, in which he states:

"Please rest assured that everything is being done to prepare this case thoroughly for trial."

With kindest regards,
Sincerely,
Paul Ross

Five or six weeks, my father thought to himself, that's when Dorothy would go in for one of her last major operations! The final pedicle, thank God, was attached now to her face. In six to seven weeks, it would be spread across and sewn on. And that had been hard to schedule. He'd have to talk it over with her, call Paul Ross, and find out what was really happening. If she went like that, with the pedicle attached to her face, everyone would see what his wife had to go through, day after day, week after week.

All he wanted was some money, the money that was overdue. Why did they have to go through a trial with everybody staring at them in court? Staring at her in particular! They had the pictures. Wasn't that enough? It was like buzzards swooping down over carrion, picking apart things that had already been injured. How could he be questioned by lawyers who would doubt his honesty, lawyers who would make him feel that the accident was his fault! He was the man, of course. How could he have let this happen to his wife? Wishing the whole thing would just go away, he went back to his book and read.

My father, who usually fell asleep easily, tossed and turned more often now. Even though he knew a faulty gas gauge had caused the accident, he still carried the guilt inside him. He was not a smooth talker or a persuasive arguer. How could he face the lawyers? He should have known better. Why did Dorothy just light the match? He should have called someone, thought more before taking action. "Look before you leap," he told the kids. "Look before you leap. Don't be so impulsive!" All these thoughts made him vulnerable to attack. He might break down and say something that would ruin the whole case. He talked with my mother about some of his fears, but she just pushed them aside, like she so often did.

"Hank, you're just making a lot out of nothing. We have a good lawyer. He'll advise us. Don't get yourself all worked up. Save your energy for the trial!"

Here she was—after another operation, her arm attached to her face—telling him to calm down.

Before my mother's last operation, her arm still attached to her face, though hidden as well as possible with a high collar and a long scarf, they got on the plane. The trip from New York to Boston was fast, and when the three of them—Paul Ross, my mother and father—arrived at the courthouse, they were shuffled into a small room where Paul briefed them again on what would happen. There were no witnesses, except Della, who had been with the children and let the gas man into the house. They had decided to take statements from her, at least in the beginning, and not call her up on the stand. The case was riding on the inspection of the gas gauge and the explosion. The gas company would first present its case to the jury and then the defense would present theirs.

"You have nothing to worry about," Paul said. "It's a clear case. I'm prepared." But my father's eyes shifted nervously from side to side and nothing my mother did or said could calm him. When they walked into the courtroom, everyone stared, especially at my mother. Even the judge, who was looking at some papers, saw her out of the corner of his eye and clutched the end of his gavel. My mother witnessed all of it. My parents and their lawyer took their places in the front left of the courtroom.

"So you see," the defense lawyer said, after talking about the evening of July 21 on Cape Cod—the dinner at the restaurant, the drink at the Fairchilds', and the drive home (with Dorothy Nayer driving)—"This is a clear case of two people drinking heavily and making a massive error in judgment. Dr. Nayer was so drunk he couldn't even drive!" The lawyer finished up with obvious character assassination: he painted a picture of two out-of-control people, drunk and stupid, who left their children while gas was being delivered at the cottage. They should have been there to supervise and not left it all up to Della Duggan.

My father's face tightened so hard, it looked like the veins would burst. Clenching his fists, he vehemently whispered to Paul that he needed to talk to him. Paul asked for a twenty-minute break and led my parents into the same small room, where my father broke down in anger and tears.

"We are not drunks! We had a total of two drinks that

night over many hours. And I hate driving at night. I have night blindness. That's common. Dorothy always drives at night. What sons of bitches!" he said, his voice rising to a fevered pitch. "And Dorothy looking like that! How could they do this to us, to her, to our children!"

"Dear, what did you expect they'd do? Of course they're going to try everything they can. They don't want to lose all that money."

"I can't stand this. I can't stand this," my father said, now up from his chair, pacing back and forth across the small room, still clenching his fists, in a state of total panic.

"Listen." Paul said. "I can try to settle out of court. I can ask for that now."

"But we'll lose money that way," my mother said.

"I don't think you'd lose much, and maybe it's better that way. Let me see what I can do. Stay here."

My mother and father sat in silence for over forty minutes, hearing people shuffling in and out of courtrooms throughout the Boston courthouse. They heard the noon siren and people going out to lunch. Sometimes they heard the sound of a gavel, and once in a while an argument or light crying in the hallways. When Paul returned, he was beaming.

"They offered $200,000 as a settlement—about twenty thousand less than I thought we'd get at the max with a trial. I think we should take it."

My parents looked at each other, both making calculations in their heads, which they had done many times before: the private schooling they wanted for their girls, the trips they might take, the medical bills, and of course the lawyer's fees.

"Give us a few minutes to think about it," my mother said.

"Goddammit, let's take it. I want to get out of this place."

"Twenty thousand dollars is a lot to lose. It could more than pay for college for both girls—and even graduate school. But I want this over, too," she said, silent for a minute, a moment of unusual vulnerability during the daylight hours.

"We'll take it," my father said. "That's a lot of money, more money than I could ever have imagined seeing in my life. But it will never be enough. Look at her. And look at me. My hands."

"Okay, I'll let them know," said Paul, "and then let's go out and celebrate."

My mother had already picked out a restaurant near the courthouse.

"Let's still spend the night and relax," she said. "We'll call Mom and Pop with the good news."

"Okay. Okay," my father replied, repeating that word to himself again and again, as if reassuring himself that everything was going to be okay, a sentiment he hadn't been able to muster up for even a second over the past three years.

After dinner, my parents strolled down one of the main streets of Boston looking at the shop windows, deciding not to notice the constant gawking of strangers.

When my mother came home, I got to the door first.

"Mommy! I'm going to sing a song at school. Grandpa just went out for a walk."

"Hi, sweetie. We must have just missed him."

"When do you go to the hospital again?"

"In three days. You can help me pick out my clothes if you want."

"Okay, Mommy, but later. I'm practicing the song."

"Daddy, Daddy, Daddy," Annie said, rushing out of the back room and throwing herself into his arms.

"Whoa," Daddy said. "Let me get my coat off first. How are you?"

"I heard there was good news," said Anne.

"Yes, good news." But that's all he said.

Two weeks later, when my mother came out of the hospital, she told Anne and me that her face was almost ready to be finished. It was being primed, like before you paint a wall. What was underneath wouldn't show once it was covered up.

Anne was excited about the new face, but was preoccupied with practicing her lines for her starring role as Amos the mouse in her fifth-grade production. She walked through the house saying her lines, sometimes shutting the back door so no one could interrupt. In the evenings Daddy helped her memorize her lines until she knew them perfectly. She would be the star of the play in a mouse costume with a tail. When Anne heard I was due to interview at a private school, she said she never wanted to leave P.S. 40.

Not long afterwards, my mother took me to the Little Red School House on Bleecker Street to "play games" with the teacher. "I'll wait for you here," Mom said as I was escorted into a colorful room. I liked the school, the smell of the green walls, and all the singing and dancing.

"Okay, Louise," a woman named Heidi said. The children all called their teachers and even the principal by their first names. "I'm going to ask you some questions. Put these beads back in the same order as you see them here."

I saw the pattern—white, pink, blue, green—and when the beads spilled into my hands, I restrung them.

"Now I'm going to ask you a question. A policeman has been shot dead. Then he gets up and goes home. What's wrong with the story?"

I thought about that question for a long time, imagining the policeman in his blue uniform lying on the ground, bleeding, screaming for help, and then? I didn't know. There was a long silence in the room as Heidi waited for me to answer. Suddenly, I flashed on the truth.

"He died, so he couldn't get up!"

The question made me feel sad, but it was the last one of the interview. That policeman kept running through my mind, again and again; I couldn't shut it off. I was confused about what dead meant, and the thought of the policeman bleeding, calling for help, disturbed me. But Heidi had not said anything about him calling for help; it was just something I heard inside my ears, like a ringing, or the constant sound of an ambulance siren.

I started attending the Little Red School House in the third grade. Although I missed some of my neighborhood friends, I loved the smell inside the small red-brick

building, the art on the walls, the sounds of music waft-
ing through the halls, the dances we learned each day,
and the frequent field trips. We did a lot of experiments
and once watched volcanoes erupt in the middle of the
classroom. We also learned the music, dances, and poems
of a new country each year. I was fortunate to attend
such a school.

My mother, too, found in this school a much smaller
world, where people didn't stare at her face. Many of
the teachers at Little Red had been blacklisted; many
were Jewish at a time of great discrimination against
Jews. Marginalized and progressive, they wanted a better
world. Some of them had lost jobs elsewhere but were
welcomed into this small and very special community,
where I would blossom for many years. My sister also
started attending school at Little Red; later the Elisabeth
Irwin High School became a haven for all of us.

The settlement came through five years after the accident.
As the papers were shuffled from one place to the next,
my parents waited for the day when our insurance company representative would bring them the check. Once
they had the check in hand, my mother would be able
plan their trip on the Queen Elizabeth to Europe, where
she had longed to go ever since she and her friend Eileen
visited Brugge and threw pennies in the fountain, wishing for handsome husbands.

Yes, she had a handsome husband and two beautiful
daughters, and she had her career. But life hadn't all gone
as planned. She wanted to feel the sea air, to go on an

adventure. So she dug up the brochures that were neatly stacked in her sewing closet, brochures she looked over from time to time, thinking about when they would leave, when the girls' school ended, how soon they would have to put down the deposit, what the actual expenses would be, and then, of course, plans for the trip itself.

They would stay with her Aunt Ivy in Exeter, who had plenty of room and had an ancient parrot that mimicked the sounds of the bombs dropping during World War II. Ivy said that Polly drove her crazy; she would be lifting a spoonful of oatmeal to her mouth when the parrot would make that terrorizing sound. But mostly Polly would just yell "Ivy!" throughout the house, repeatedly calling "Ivy! Ivy!" She also had a cross-eyed cat, Dinky, who followed her up and down the stairs. In the afternoons, Ivy loved to go to the moors, which were covered with purple heather, and sit among the cows and paint. The girls would love seeing Ivy, their grandmother's cousin. Of course, they would also visit the cousins in Thorverton and view the town of thatched roofs and two shops where her grandmother had lived for seventeen years. They would also have an adventure in London, seeing the museums and a play or two (*The Mousetrap*, without question), and indulging in a two-night stay in the Savoy, one of the fanciest hotels in all of London.

My mother took a deep breath as she flipped through the Cunard Line brochure. But then she put it back in the stack of papers, and began neatly packing her travel suitcase for her last operation. The suitcase was beginning to get worn after more than thirty-five trips to the hospital. She didn't want to have this done, to be out of commission for two weeks again, the girls home without her, the anesthesia, the grogginess, the pain, the silent terror. But this was to be the last operation, the crowning glory, when the skin would finally be moved from the pedicle to her face. Her whole face would now be covered with snow-white skin from her stomach. Like Sleeping Beauty, dark hair and white skin. Her hair used to be blonde and then light brown, but it had grown dark after the fire. Perhaps she would even look better, she mused to herself, with such soft skin from her tummy. People would turn to look at her because she was pretty, not because she was burned. Every once in a while she felt scared thinking of the anesthesia, the danger, the final face. Would she be disappointed? She pushed that thought far away. No use dwelling on the negative. Hank did enough of that for the both of them. But in the past few days, at odd times, her stomach had clenched and sent her running to the bathroom. She didn't want to go to the hospital again, to leave Anne and Louise and her house. She didn't want to go under the knife.

That morning when my mother was due to go to the hospital, our apartment assumed its familiar, quiet air of terror.

"Hi, Mommy," I said.

"Hi, sweetie. Good morning. We're going to leave in a few minutes. Remember about your homework. And listen to Daddy. You can talk with me in a few days."

"Not tomorrow, Mommy? I can't talk to you then?"

"No, remember, this is the big operation. I'll need a few days to recover."

I stood there in my pajamas and slippers, scratching

the backs of my legs, which suddenly itched. Our neighbor Bunny was there to help us get ready for school. My mother went into the hall closet, which smelled of winter wool, and got out her red coat. My father picked up her suitcase, so preoccupied that he almost forgot to say good-bye to me or to Anne, who had run down the hallway to join us.

"Bye, Mommy, good luck," Anne said, hugging our parents. Then she ran back to her room to get ready for school.

I put my arms around my mother and didn't let go until she pried my arms from around her waist.

"Now go back and get dressed. Make sure you brush your teeth. Give them a good brushing. We have to go," she said, staring at me for a bit too long as I went off to the bathroom. Then she gestured to my father to move out the door.

That day, when I came home from school, I went to Playground Number Two and raced across the gray concrete, back and forth, back and forth. Sometimes I tried to skin my knees so that I could see drops of blood trickling down my shins and later pick off the scabs that formed. Finally, when no one was looking, I ran fast across the ground, made myself slip, and landed extra hard on my knee. The ground was rougher than I thought, and my thin cotton pants tore, blood oozing out between the light, blue threads.

"What did you do that for!" Anne exclaimed, coming out from behind the slide.

"It hurts, Annie, my knee really hurts."

Annie sat next to me on the bench and even put her hand on my forehead like she had done at the farm. I cried into her white cotton shirt.

"Let's go upstairs," she said, "and put a Band-Aid on your cut." She took me by the hand and led me to the elevator. Anne cleaned my cut and helped me find some new pants to wear. Then she pulled me aside.

"I saw you do that to yourself. Why?"

"I don't know. Sometimes I do that. Don't tell anybody. Okay?"

"Okay."

While I waited anxiously for my mother to return, I thought about another time when she'd returned from the hospital: She walked into the house with her face and scalp completely bandaged, looking like a mummy with two slits for eyes and an opening for her mouth. At that moment, I wished my mother would go away, lie down on her twin bed in her room across from the linen closet and disappear, only to reappear beautiful, like the Hollywood stars that the plastic surgeons were modeling her after. I didn't want any friends over. I hated the antiseptic smell that swept through the house. That night, at the dinner table, Mommy picked up her fork and put mashed potatoes into the mouth hole. It was all because soon she would be beautiful. Soon she would be beautiful. The bandages wrapped around and around her face would soon be taken off. After dinner, when her face was still bandaged, I noticed the holes for her nostrils. For ten days the bandages stayed on. I dreamed that the whole world had been wrapped up and I would never find out what was inside.

Before her return from the hospital this time, Annie and I talked to her often on the phone. As usual, Daddy often seemed preoccupied. He came home at 7:00 p.m., read a few books to us, and drifted off to sleep on the black-and-white armchair in the living room. I missed Della. My mother didn't want a "live-in" anymore and had gone in search of someone who could come every day. We had a few different babysitters during that last operation.

Our new housekeeper, Evelyn Baines, took us into the back room after our baths so we wouldn't wake our father. While my mother was in the hospital, Evelyn had agreed to stay and help us get ready for bed for the weeks that my mother would be in the hospital. She had started coming every day; Evelyn, with her strong, calm presence, would stay with our family for more than thirty years.

At 4:00 p.m. on the day that my mother was to return, I pressed my face against the windowpane. Just as I had always thrown up on that one spot at my aunt and uncle's farm, that one small patch of linoleum with the gold sparkles that would circle like my stomach circled, I had one patch of windowpane where I always looked out for my mother, like a lighthouse keeper. Every day, I would stand by the window in the living room, making sure the long, beige curtains were parted perfectly for me to retrieve my spot, and stare out at the serpentine road that I knew my mother would take to our building. On many days, I would see women in red coats like my mother's pushing shopping carts, talking with friends, or just sauntering along the gray concrete path of Peter

Cooper. But once their faces turned toward me, I knew they weren't my mother. They hadn't been burned.

Today was different. I knew my mom could be any of those women with doughy skin spread over their faces like a thin, milky batter. I wanted to see the face I would grow into. I couldn't remember my mother's face before the accident, only the way she smelled and the feel of her crocheted lavender shawl brushing my cheeks on the night she and my dad went to the play on Cape Cod.

Suddenly my heart beat faster and I rubbed my icy fingers together, trying to get the circulation going. I took a deep breath. It looked like her, the same red woolen coat, the same black patent leather purse, the same walk, the same height, the same movement of the legs across the road. But from two stories above and the figure still so far away, I couldn't see the face, the final face.

Instinctively, I put my hands up to my own cheeks and felt the softness of my skin. Then I felt my heart drop two stories to the ground. My mother had lifted up her face, as if searching for her daughters, and it was fat and strange, like somebody had put Silly Putty over her, blobby like the fat-faced sculpture that I had just made in the art room at Little Red, a round circle of flesh. But this was from two stories above. How could I really see? I'd have to wait until my mother entered the apartment.

When I heard the key turn in the door, I was scared, so I walked slowly out to the living room, my hands stuck stiffly in the pockets of my blue jeans. My mother was looking at the mail. Only Evelyn was in the house, quietly cleaning in the back. When my mother lifted up her face, it was the same blobby flesh I had seen out the window. My heart dropped again. The skin wasn't spread thinly across her face; it was a big glob. I wanted to tell my mother that she looked great, just like in the picture of her on her wedding day: the beautiful face, the strong chin. But it wasn't true.

"Your face looks puffy," I said, all my hope shattered.

"Hi sweetie," she said, coming toward me, inspecting me after the two weeks away and giving me a hug and a kiss. "Yes, it is puffy. Actually, that's fat under the skin. I'll have to go back one or two more times. They can suck the fat out. It's called defatting. But I'll need to go into the hospital for that. They gave me a little chin."

I saw two crisscrossed lines sewn into the bottom of a blob of flesh that was now her chin. "I see, Mommy," I said, trying very hard to be cheerful.

She looked tired and started sorting through the mail.

"We're having lamb chops for dinner," she said. "Your favorite."

"Oh good, Mommy," I said, not looking directly at her.

I then went to the bathroom and looked at my face in the mirror. My eyes started to tear, so I threw cold water on my face to stop the feeling. I looked up again and saw my high cheekbones and dark eyes. I was pretty; I looked nothing like my mother. I prayed I never would.

The day before the insurance men came to deliver the check, my mother rode the bus uptown and bought a meat slicer. She would prepare turkey sandwiches on rye bread, salad, French fries, and an assortment of drinks. The turkey had to be sliced perfectly. The house would be cleaned. Yes, she would make a proper lunch for them before they handed her the check. While my father was at work and we were at school, Evelyn would help her set the table and put out the serving plates. She would wear a new outfit she had bought, a red woolen skirt and white silk shirt. Perhaps she wouldn't wear a scarf, as she was beginning to go out without a scarf, and the silk shirt had a nice, wide collar.

The morning of February 3, 1959, she spent a long time penciling in her eyebrows and putting on her thick pancake makeup, especially over the lines where the new skin had been sewn onto her cheeks. Just last week, for the first time, she had been able to answer the question "When is the doctor going to make you look like you were before, Mommy?" with "Never." She had accepted the truth, herself. Now she focused on the check, which she envisioned being handed to her with a handshake. She thought of the Little Red School House and the trip she wanted to take. Perhaps they would have been able to afford private schools without this money, but they never would have taken a trip on the Queen Elizabeth, a luxury liner. She would go right to the bank when the insurance men left. She wouldn't want a check of that size sitting in the house for too long. The check was for her face, for her husband's wounds, and for all the collateral damage to their lives. The check was the culmination of years of waiting. Now they would put the accident behind them. They had to do that. They all had to move on with their lives.

The doorbell rang. Two middle-aged men, both pleasant enough, entered the Peter Cooper apartment to a spread of food they had not expected. Their eyes glanced quickly at my mother's face and hands but then rested on the meal spread out before them. This was the trick. She had succeeded.

My mother, in her usual curious way, got them both to talk about their families, where they went to school, where they lived. After thirty minutes went by, everyone stopped talking. One of the men reached for his briefcase and pulled out some papers and a check. My mother, anticipating this moment, had a pen nearby. She signed her name on three pages, dated the forms, and was handed the check. After the men left the house, Evelyn cleaned up the dishes and my mother went to the bank with visions of the whole family, the four of them, on the deck of the Queen Elizabeth, crossing the Atlantic Ocean to a new land, to her mother's home, to England's green and promised land.

In late July of 1959, we boarded the Queen Elizabeth, exactly five years after the fire. My father, as usual, was anxious, but he was also overwhelmed by the beauty of the ship with its long decks. Our cabin was small, cabin class, below deck, with four bunk beds and a porthole through which we could see the ocean water sweeping across the glass. Annie and I had new clothes: I had a blue-and-white-checked dress with a red rose brocaded on the front; Anne, a pink-and-white-checked dress with a soft, white collar. We felt rich and special on such a big ship.

The first night, while the ship was still in port, we had Baked Alaska for dessert, a huge, sugary cake topped with ice cream and encased in meringue. When the waiter struck a match and lit the meringue on fire, I instinctively moved away. My mother clapped her hands and my father looked in astonishment. Anne and I inhaled the sugary smell and watched the waiter cut off the luxurious slices. I had my fork ready by the time my plate was set down.

Before the horse races began in half an hour, when Annie and I would bet shillings on the little wooden horses, we would all go out on deck. The sun had gone down while we were finishing our main course. When we were inside, we only felt the subtle movements of the sea, like babies floating in amniotic fluid, rocking only slightly back and forth through the dark water. Now the waves were slapping against the great cruise liner.

My sister was out the door first, her white cardigan buttoned over her shoulders; when the cool breeze hit, she put her arms inside the sleeves. My mother and father followed her, and then I followed them out the door, the skirt of my white-and-blue-checked dress blowing up slightly. Embarrassed, I pressed my hands on the shiny cotton and held them there, looking around to make sure no one had seen. We all walked over to the railing and looked out at the water. We breathed deeply, more deeply than we had breathed in months, entranced by the phosphorescence of the endless Atlantic. Soon we would go in to the horse races. Then we would all go to sleep on the bunk beds in our small cabin, the sound and motion of the sea rocking us to sleep, up and down, all of us together. In five days we would see the white cliffs of Dover.

We had come so far, journeyed so many thousands of miles to get to this very moment. My mother's face turned toward the ocean, her hands in her pockets.

Epilogue

My mother died on July 21, 2001, at the age of ninety-one. She lived a long and full life after the accident, working as an editor for the *American Journal of Nursing*, writing articles for an English nursing journal, and mentoring countless student nurses in her determination to change the field. She also helped to unionize her office, demanding that everyone talk openly about their salaries so inequities could be corrected.

Wherever she went, she made friends and kept them until the day she died. She continued to write thank-you cards and letters of condolence. She cared endlessly about other people and their lives, collecting pictures of babies and pets she would never meet again, but whose names she always remembered.

She was vivacious and "kept all her buttons" until the end. She was also an inveterate traveler, always planning the next adventure and making sure to get my father to go along with her. She desperately wanted to go on the Queen Elizabeth 2, and in her wheelchair, at eighty years old, she boarded the namesake of the ship we had ridden so many years before.

Despite her deformed hands, including the one doctors had long ago declared "no longer useful," she sewed suits, dresses, and shirts for herself and for others. She took classes at the French Fashion Institute and smocked a dress for my daughter, Sarah, and a small trench coat lined with plaid.

These achievements, both large and small, are a testimony to her extraordinary strength and her staunch will. Yet she was also a woman who could be difficult, free with criticism and extremely stingy with praise. She had a "right way" to do things. In the last years, she and my father often bickered. "Hank," she would demand from another room, "bring me my tea." Once when I visited her, I didn't push the chair back correctly in front of the desk, and she got very upset with me. I can't remember her ever saying "I'm sorry." Looking back, there were many instances of never measuring up that were like a hole in my heart. At the best moments, though, I could respond to her strength with humor and shed the skin of the wounded little girl.

At the very end of her life, Anne and I both talked to her every day on the phone and visited her often. By then she had softened. Even her face had softened.

"Our goal was to give you and Anne as normal a life as possible despite how we looked or felt," she said in a letter she sent to me when I was writing this book. Only after raising my own children would I fully realize the enormity of that undertaking.

My father died two years after my mother, having endured a long and difficult period on a skilled nursing floor. He briefly thought of calling The Hemlock Society, wanting to choose to die once my mother was gone. But he decided to carry on, much as he had many years ago, after the accident. We read him poetry: Yeats, Whitman, and Rumi, among others. Once, when I mistook the name of an author, he pulled himself up from his sleeping position and corrected me. He, too, kept his sharp intellect until the end. He could also be abrupt and continued to struggle with depression, asking God why he was still alive after my mother died, just as he had raised his fists to God after the accident, asking "Why me?"

Though he was humble and did not talk much about his accomplishments, they were many: medical officer of the New York City Fire Department, president of the New York Lung Association, a founder of Health Insurance Plan, a beloved doctor, a member of Phi Beta Kappa, and a Renaissance man who was endlessly curious about the world. At his retirement party at the fire department, the men all rose and gave him a standing ovation, the first ever for one of their doctors.

Being with him, even at the very end of his life, was an adventure because of his vast knowledge of so many subjects, ranging from politics to poetry. He was a lover of Shakespeare, Freud, and mathematics. In his own way, he fought for a better world. He helped countless patients during the McCarthy era, protecting them from being hounded by the FBI, charging lower rates for office visits, and sometimes accepting paintings and sculptures as payment from those who had no money. Most importantly, he and my mother loved each other deeply. "We stayed together and loved each other," my father said about my mother. "And that, I'm sure, was important for you and Anne."

Some years after Annie and I left the farm, Uncle Louis and his family bought a house in Norwich, New York, which he tended to with great pride. He worked as a stationary engineer for Norwich Pharmacy until his retirement. He continued to spend as much time as he could with his family, and he was proud of his children and grandchildren. Just before retirement, he and Aunt Rusty bought a trailer and a piece of property by a lake. Sadly, he died at the age of sixty, and it was one of the only times I ever saw my mother cry. He loved his children, Jean and Robert, and his five grandchildren. Though he had not been interested in school as a young person, he valued education and both his children went on to earn graduate degrees. On one visit after his first heart attack, he told me how good he felt about his life. He continued to be a family man to the end, cooking roast beef dinners and grilling food for family and friends.

When Uncle Louis died, Aunt Rusty struggled terribly. She had always been dependent on my uncle. She had never learned to drive. It was a difficult time for her, but she spent many hours nurturing her grandchildren as she had nurtured her children and Anne and me. She also got a dog. Her house was a haven of warmth for many people, young and old. She kept pictures of Anne and me on her bureau until the day she died. In her heart, Anne and I remained her children.

My cousin Jean, with whom Anne and I endlessly romped in the fields during the months we lived on the farm, got married soon after college. She and her husband, John, lived in upstate New York for many years in a beautiful home that Jean helped design. She became a special education teacher and had two sons. Eventually, they left upstate New York and now live in a beautiful area of Tennessee where cows roam nearby. Despite suffering from health problems, both she and John are involved in their community. Jean continues to do what she can with grace, intelligence, and determination.

Robert also married young, and he and his wife, Madeline, live in North Carolina. He always kept in close touch with my parents, who, he says, inspired him and his wife to be great adventurers in life. Recently, they traveled to Europe and Morocco. After a career with the phone company, Robert was a math professor for a time. Now he spends his time fly-fishing, teaching young people about the outdoors, and doing community service. He and Madeline have two sons, one daughter, and two beloved grandchildren. Robert once wrote to me, "You were my sister for a short and precious time."

Stella Chess died in March 2007. She had an illustrious career as a psychiatrist and with her husband did groundbreaking work helping parents to understand that they need to adjust to their child's temperament and that children are simply different, not "good" or "bad." When I started writing this book and first approached her, I was having severe panic attacks. She acknowledged my mother's strength and my father's depression. Later on, we spoke at length and she described my parents as "good patients" who listened to most of the advice that she had given to them. Still, my mother was dead set against being in therapy herself or having her children seen by a professional, so there was only so much Stella could do. She also told me that she encouraged my parents to pick us up sooner, but that my mother felt her looks would be too frightening to us. I'll never be sure exactly what happened because my mother had said, "I was not going to do what other people told me to do. You needed to be picked up." What is important is that my father did come for us, and we became a family again.

For Anne, the turbulent sixties, combined with depression, unexplored post-traumatic stress, and buried scars, conspired to make life difficult. She became a social worker and worked tirelessly with people from all walks of life, witnessing a lot of suffering and a lot of redemption. Recently, she returned to her tropical home in St. Thomas with her teenage daughter, Lily, and has become more "pre-accident" every day; she is painting, playing music, and setting up her life-coaching business to help empower people to live their dreams as she is now doing. Over time, she has awakened to the fact that she is a Renaissance woman and an adventurer. Perhaps for Anne, getting younger at heart is a function of her growing older. Perhaps it is a shedding of a hardened skin that protected a sensitive soul, the wounded little girl who had once been abandoned. Anne and I talk endlessly on the phone. We are so distant from each other geographically, but we remain so close.

I, like Anne, went on a turbulent journey in the sixties, working to change the world and trying to find my place in it. As a student I joined anti-war protests, and later campaigned for a black studies department at the

University of Wisconsin-Madison; I always tried to fight for a more equitable world. Today I am a tenured professor at City College of San Francisco, where I teach classes in English composition, literature, and creative writing. I have published two books of poetry and one book of nonfiction, and I have found the writing of this book to be a powerful journey.

My husband, Jim, and I have been married for more than twenty-four years and we have two wonderful daughters who are creative, loving, and smart. I also have a wonderful stepdaughter, son-in-law, and three grandchildren living in Connecticut whom we visit every summer. Years ago, and with help from my parents, we bought a home in San Francisco, which Jim tends to lovingly. I still struggle with anxiety, especially in small elevators, the old terror rearing its head as if I were four again. The hurtling of cars and the odors of exhaust fumes remind me that I might burn in all that fire. But now I cross the Bay Bridge with ease. On many days, I play my self-hypnosis tapes, and I continue to see a therapist. I find many moments of pure joy.

Anne and I and our parents spent many years of our lives connected to each other by wires and scars, by a black telephone cord, by the cadence and sounds of a constant and painful reality. That we left out too much for too long is a given. That Anne and I bear the scars is a fact. That the four of us ultimately said most of what we needed to say to each other is the final gift.

Anne and I are twin souls, not only because we were born into the same family. Like the *hibakusha* (victims of the atomic bombing) of Hiroshima, we share an experience that can't be easily understood by others. On the outside, we are everything that the children of successful professionals should be. That we struggle a bit more, hug our children too hard when we say good-bye for the evening, or become too quiet too quickly makes us, at the very best, "complicated." But we have gotten the help and love we've needed to continue to change and grow, to climb step by step out of that incendiary cellar.

Acknowledgements

This book has been a long journey with numerous people helping me in a myriad of ways. Thank you also to those whose names are not mentioned below.

For research: The Wellfleet Fire Department which provided me with the alarm record from 1954; the Provincetown Playhouse for researching the play my parents saw the night of the accident; my parents' friends, Penny Speckter and Shirley Fondiller for letters, anecdotes, insights and endless support; my writing groups and other writers including editing by Rose Heller, Leslie Lingaas, Kathryn Olney, Shannon Barton Wren, Debbie Osborne, Susan Eisenberg and Myrna Chapman.

Special thanks to those who shaped the book: Sydelle Kramer, Olga Zundel, Jim Eilers, Ginny Lang, Dixie Morse, Jeri McGovern, Ken Silver and particularly to Martin Kevan who worked with me over many months to expand and mold the story.

To Laurie Bernstein: You made this happen with your energy and expertise and always believed in the story and in my writing; to Jim Atlas and all those at Atlas and Co., thank you for giving this book the perfect home and especially to my editor, Nataša Lekić whose grace and wisdom guided me through the final stages; to my step-daughter, Bonnie, for helping me get the book into the right hands and for believing it would get published; to my daughters, Sarah and Laura, thank you for bringing me back to the present moment, for all your love and editing help and for putting up with me; to my sister who always listened, gave me endless suggestions and insights and allowed me to plumb the depths of that difficult time with her even when it was hard; and finally to my husband, Jim Patten, who listened to me, gave me invaluable editing suggestions, and loved me without ceasing through this story and now for the new stories to come.